Unshakeable: Self-Love Beyond the Male Gaze

Copyright © 2025

No part of this publication may be reproduced, stored in a retrieval system, or transmitted in any form or by any means, electronic, mechanical, photocopying, recording, or otherwise, without the prior written permission of the publisher.

Printed in the United States of America

First Edition: 2025

This copyright page includes the necessary copyright notice, permissions request information, acknowledgments for the cover design, interior design, and editing, as well as the details of the first edition.

Disclaimer: This book is a work of non-fiction and is intended solely for informational and educational purposes. The names mentioned within are trademarks of their respective owners. This publication is not affiliated with, endorsed by, or sponsored by any of these trademark holders. The inclusion of these names is meant to provide context and historical reference.

The author does not claim ownership of any trademarks or copyrights related to the names and likenesses of the individuals referenced in this book. Any opinions expressed herein are those of the author and do not necessarily reflect the views of any organization or trademark holder.

Introduction

There are mornings when the bright, sharp light of day seems to expose every flaw we imagine about ourselves. Before we even leave our bedrooms, we stand in front of mirrors, cataloging the bumps, lines, and curves that don't quite match what we saw scrolling through our phones the night before. It would be easy to believe we are supposed to be someone else—someone more flawless, thinner, more attractive, or more "worthy." That sneaky tug at our confidence—often so familiar we barely notice it—has roots deeper than we might think.

Growing up, the idea that our worth is measured by how others, especially men, see us is everywhere. Movies, advertisements, and social media bombard us with the message: beauty equals value. Sometimes the words aren't even spoken aloud. A look, a comment, or the absence of attention can lodge itself under the skin, whispering doubts that stick for years. Research by the Dove Self-Esteem Project found that 54% of girls worldwide don't think they're beautiful—nearly half of the girls you pass in the hallway, sit beside in class, or see posting selfies. The pressure to "fit" is heavier than a backpack stuffed with textbooks.

And yet, something inside us pushes back. That quiet voice that insists we are more than what we look like. More than a snap judgment in someone else's eyes. When 15-year-old Alina wore her favorite bright yellow dress to a family party, she was met with offhand comments about how "bold" she looked, or whether she was "trying to attract attention." That night, she cried in her room, wondering if she had made a mistake, if her self-assurance was misplaced. But, after many journal entries and a few heart-to-hearts with friends, Alina slowly began to realize her sense of worth could not be held hostage to outside opinions. She started to ask, "What would it feel like... if 'enough' came from inside me, not from the faces around me?"

Unshakeable self-love grows from nurturing this kind of inner strength. It is not noisy. It does not depend on winning approval, nor does it fade when the noise of outside judgment quiets. Consider the words of Dr. Brené Brown, who said, "Owning our story and loving ourselves through that process is the bravest thing that we will ever do." True self-love means celebrating who we are even when no one else notices, understanding that we deserve kindness simply because we exist.

It's a tall order, of course, to stop caring what others think completely. We are social beings. Compliments still feel good, while criticism can sting for days. Psychologists call this "external validation," and it shapes us from childhood. Little kids beam when praised for a new dress or haircut; teenagers blossom under a cute crush's smile. No one is immune to the rush of being noticed, and there is nothing wrong with enjoying positive attention. The trouble comes when that attention becomes the only currency for feeling good. Instead of collecting compliments as little boosts along the way, some people begin to crave them like air.

What often trips us up is the "male gaze." This isn't just a fancy term from a college class; it's a real force built into our culture. The male gaze describes how society tends to view women through a lens that centers men's desires and opinions. Whether it's movies focusing on a girl's body as if she's on display, or even everyday comments about appearance, the message is clear: your value is tied to being looked at and approved of by men. Over time, it can be easy to forget what you truly like about yourself outside of that lens.

For a long time, this way of seeing the world has shaped the stories girls are told and tell themselves. As author Naomi Wolf observed, "A culture fixated on female thinness is not an obsession about female beauty but an obsession about female obedience." The standards shift, but the core message remains: conform, fit in, or fade away. Many young women spend years perfecting poses for pictures, changing how they laugh, and shrinking themselves so that they don't stand out 'the wrong way.' It's exhausting, and it can steal not just joy but also time and potential.

But the ability to rewrite our own narrative is powerful. Maya Angelou once wrote, "If you are always trying to be normal, you will never know how amazing you can be." Imagine if the energy spent worrying about how you are seen could be rerouted—poured into new skills, friendships, adventures, and passions. If the soundtrack in your head played tunes of self-confidence instead of self-doubt, what might you try that you've avoided out of fear? The process of learning to love yourself for real, not just in motivational slogans, is radical work. It shakes loose the belief that your value is up for public vote.

Learning this lesson doesn't happen overnight. Some days, you may feel truly unstoppable; other days, a single unkind remark can drag you back into old patterns. That's normal. Building a heart that can weather both storms and sunshine is a process—a mixture of curiosity, patience, and being far kinder to yourself than our culture ever encouraged. Dr. Kristin Neff, who pioneered research on self-compassion, puts it this way: "With self-compassion, we give ourselves the same kindness and care we'd give to a good friend."

Take a look at the world around you. From Instagram feeds to TikTok trends, it can seem like everyone else has cracked the code to confidence. But often, those perfect posts hide silent battles with insecurity. In a 2022 survey by the American Psychological Association, 61% of girls aged 14 to 17 said social media made them feel pressure to look a certain way. Even influencers, whose lives seem picture-perfect, have spoken openly about filtering not just their photos, but their feelings as well.

Yet community and connection can offer something the trend cycle cannot: a sense of belonging not built on looks. When friends lift each other up, when stories of vulnerability are shared, those walls of self-doubt start to crumble. Actress and activist Jameela Jamil, founder of the "I Weigh" movement, believes in "valuing yourself in numbers that the scale can't measure." These are the friendships and spaces where laughter is loudest, where inside jokes become armor, and where mistakes are simply part of being alive.

Cultivating self-love means getting practical, too. There are tools—both old and new—that can help us quiet the harsh inner critic and accentuate the gentler, wiser voice inside. For some, it's journaling about daily wins and challenges. For others, it's repeating affirmations until they begin to feel true. Mindfulness, movement, art, music—each can teach you to be present with yourself, without judgment. It's about carving out time and space to ask: "How am I, really?" And then listening to the answer.

Of course, the journey of self-love is not only about feeling good all the time. Sometimes, it's messy. Setting boundaries, saying no, removing yourself from toxic situations—these are acts of courage that take practice. At first, standing up for your own needs may feel selfish or strange. Over time, though, the act of drawing your own lines transforms from uncomfortable to empowering. As you learn to honor your feelings, you'll also discover that those who truly respect you will honor them as well.

Even in the closest relationships, the challenge of holding onto your sense of self remains. Whether with friends, family members, or romantic partners, being honest about what you want—and don't want—can feel risky. But communicating with compassion and clarity is what keeps your sense of self strong. It unlocks the possibility for connection based on mutual respect, not fear or people-pleasing. When you show up as your real self, you invite others to do the same.

Real change comes in small, consistent steps. Each time you choose self-care over self-criticism, reflection over reactivity, you water the roots of unshakeable self-love. You discover that you are enough, right now—not five pounds lighter, not with clearer skin or longer hair, not with a boyfriend or more followers. Your beauty cannot be captured in a number or a filter.

Why should you care about self-love beyond the male gaze? Because your life is too precious to be spent shrinking yourself for someone else's comfort. Because the world—messy, complicated, beautiful as it is—needs more people living boldly, not quietly apologizing for who they are. Your sense of self-worth sets the tone for every choice you make, every relationship you enter, and every risk you're willing to take. It's not about waiting to be chosen; it's about choosing yourself, every single day.

There is an old story about a pottery maker who repairs broken vases with gold. Instead of hiding the cracks, they fill them with shimmer, making the vessel stronger and more beautiful. Scars become part of the masterpiece. In much the same way, every struggle you've had with your body, every doubt or harsh word you've internalized, becomes part of a unique mosaic—the story of you, whole and worthy, just as you are.

As you move through these pages, remember that the goal isn't perfection, but wholeness. The questions you ask matter. The kindness you offer yourself matters. At the end of the day, the world will always have opinions. The only one you truly need to live with is the one that comes from within. Unshakeable self-love is not a destination you reach, but a daily invitation—a promise that no one can take away.

Table of Contents

Chapter 1: Unfiltered Reflections – The Challenge and Promise of Body Positivity Today
- Defining Body Positivity: Origins, Evolution, and Current Meaning
- The Realities of Modern Body Image Struggles
- Media, Social Media, and the Double-Edged Sword
- Intersectionality: How Race, Gender, and Ability Shape the Conversation
- Pragmatic Body Positivity: Bridging the Gap Between Acceptance and Action

Chapter 2: Beyond the Mirror – Understanding the Male Gaze and Its Impact on Self-Worth
- Defining the Male Gaze: Origins and Societal Influence
- How Media Shapes Perceptions of Beauty and Value
- Internalizing the Gaze: Effects on Self-Esteem and Body Image
- Breaking the Cycle: Recognizing and Challenging External Validation
- Practical Steps for Cultivating Self-Worth from Within

Chapter 3: Internalizing Confidence – Where External Validation Begins and Ends
- Distinguishing External Validation from Internal Self-Worth
- Recognizing Healthy vs. Unhealthy Validation-Seeking
- Shifting from Approval-Seeking to Self-Affirmation
- Building Lasting Confidence Through Personal Achievements
- Practical Exercises for Fostering Internal Confidence

Chapter 4: Rewriting Your Inner Narrative – The Power of Self-Talk
- Understanding Your Current Inner Narrative: Identifying Patterns in Self-Talk
- The Science Behind Self-Talk: How Words Shape Beliefs and Behaviors
- Uncovering Negative Self-Talk: Recognizing and Challenging Inner Criticisms
- Techniques for Rewriting Your Narrative: Transforming Self-Talk into Empowerment
- Sustaining Change: Making Positive Self-Talk a Daily Habit

Chapter 5: Male Attention Decoded – Types, Triggers, and Emotional Responses
- Categories of Male Attention: From Friendly to Romantic to Superficial
- What Triggers Male Interest: Psychological, Social, and Biological Factors
- Decoding Subtle Versus Overt Signals of Male Attention
- Emotional Reactions: How Men Feel and Express Interest
- Myths and Misunderstandings: Common Misinterpretations of Male Signals

Chapter 6: Turning Criticism into Compassion – Handling Negative or Unwanted Attention
- Understanding the Nature of Criticism—Intentions Versus Impact
- Emotional Self-Regulation in the Face of Negative Attention
- Reframing Criticism: Developing Empathy for Others' Perspectives
- Communicating with Compassion: How to Respond Rather Than React
- Transforming Personal Growth Through Constructive Handling of Criticism

Chapter 7: When Compliments Complicate – Navigating Positive Attention Without Losing Yourself
- Understanding the Double-Edged Sword of Compliments: Why Positive Attention Can Feel Unsettling
- Distinguishing Between Genuine Praise and Manipulation: Reading Intentions Behind Compliments
- Staying Grounded: Strategies for Maintaining Authenticity Amid Positive Recognition
- Setting Healthy Boundaries: Accepting Praise Without Feeling Obligated
- Turning Compliments Into Connection: Responding Effectively Without Losing Yourself

Chapter 8: Cultivating Self-Compassion – Practical Tools for Healing and Growth
- Understanding Self-Compassion: Breaking Down Myths and Misconceptions
- Recognizing and Challenging the Inner Critic
- Practical Exercises for Building Self-Kindness

- The Role of Mindfulness in Self-Compassion
- Integrating Self-Compassion into Everyday Life

Chapter 9: Journal as Sanctuary – Transforming Experiences into Empowerment
- Understanding the Journal as a Safe Haven
- Processing Raw Emotions and Difficult Memories
- Shifting Perspective—Reframing Experiences Through Writing
- Identifying Patterns: From Pain Points to Personal Growth
- Transforming Insights into Actionable Empowerment

Chapter 10: Setting Boundaries – Claiming Your Space with Grace and Strength
- Understanding the Importance of Boundaries—Why They Matter for Well-Being
- Identifying Your Limits—Recognizing Where You Need Space
- Communicating Boundaries Assertively and Respectfully
- Navigating Pushback—Responding to Boundary Violations with Confidence
- Sustaining Healthy Boundaries—Maintaining Consistency Over Time

Chapter 11: From Reaction to Response – Mindfulness Practices for Reframing
- Understanding the Difference: Reaction vs. Response
- The Science of Mindfulness and Its Impact on Emotional Regulation
- Core Mindfulness Techniques for Creating Space Between Stimulus and Action
- Practical Exercises: Training the Mind to Pause and Reframe
- Real-Life Applications: Turning Triggers into Opportunities for Thoughtful Response

Chapter 12: Community over Comparison – Leveraging Social Media for Inspiration, Not Insecurity
- Understanding the Comparison Trap: How Social Media Shapes Our Self-Perception
- Spotting Signals: Identifying Content That Uplifts vs. Content That Drains
- Curating Your Feed for Inspiration: Practical Steps to Build a Positive Online Space

- Building Genuine Connections: Engaging with Communities Rather Than Competitors
- Transforming Envy into Empowerment: Turning Inspiration into Action

Chapter 13: Building a Body Positive Mindset – Affirmations and Rituals That Last
- Understanding the Foundations of Body Positivity
- Identifying and Challenging Negative Self-Talk
- Crafting Personalized Body Positive Affirmations
- Designing Daily Rituals for Lasting Mindset Shifts
- Measuring Progress and Celebrating Self-Growth

Chapter 14: Saying Yes to Yourself – Self-Care as Radical Self-Love
- Redefining Self-Care: Moving Beyond Superficial Acts
- Understanding Self-Love as an Act of Defiance
- Identifying and Challenging Internalized Barriers to Self-Care
- Developing a Personalized Self-Care Practice Rooted in Self-Compassion
- Cultivating Consistency: Integrating Radical Self-Love into Daily Life

Chapter 15: Confidence in Action – Showing Up Authentically Everywhere
- Understanding Authenticity: What It Means to Show Up as Yourself
- Identifying and Overcoming Barriers to Authentic Self-Expression
- Cultivating Self-Awareness to Strengthen Confidence
- Practical Strategies for Bringing Your True Self into Different Settings
- Maintaining Authenticity in the Face of Judgment or Rejection

Chapter 16: Navigating Relationships – Communicating Boundaries and Desires with Partners
- Understanding Personal Boundaries and Desires
- Identifying and Articulating Your Needs
- Active Listening and Mutual Respect in Conversations
- Managing Disagreements and Setting Limits
- Building Ongoing Communication Habits with Partners

Chapter 17: Role Models and Reality – Learning from Body Positive Influencers
- Defining Body Positivity in the Social Media Era
- Spotlight on Influencers: Diverse Voices and Lived Experiences
- Breaking Myths: What Authentic Body Positivity Looks Like
- Navigating Social Media: Balancing Inspiration with Reality
- Translating Inspiration into Daily Life: Practical Strategies for Self-Acceptance

Chapter 18: Moving from Surviving to Thriving – Anchoring Confidence in Everyday Life
- Recognizing the Shift: Signs You're Ready to Move Beyond Survival Mode
- Reframing Daily Challenges as Opportunities for Growth
- Cultivating Confidence Through Small, Consistent Actions
- Building Supportive Environments That Encourage Thriving
- Celebrating Progress and Sustaining Momentum

Chapter 19: Becoming a Beacon – Inspiring Others and Owning Your Story
- Understanding the Power of Personal Narrative
- Embracing Vulnerability to Create Genuine Connections
- Transforming Challenges into Points of Inspiration
- Amplifying Your Impact: Sharing Your Story Responsibly
- Encouraging and Empowering Others to Share Their Own Journeys

Chapter 20: Unshakeable – Crafting Your Everlasting Foundation of Self-Love
- Reflecting on the Journey: Revisiting Key Lessons in Self-Love
- Identifying and Honoring Your Core Values
- Establishing Daily Rituals to Reinforce Self-Acceptance
- Sustaining Growth: Navigating Setbacks with Compassion
- Embracing a Lifelong Commitment to Yourself

Chapter 1

For as long as people have gathered around mirrors, magazines, or smartphone screens, questions about bodies—how they look, how they should feel—have lingered like a persistent echo. Sometimes quiet, sometimes blaring, but always present. Everyone has a body, and yet, how each person sees and treats theirs can differ wildly. Standing at the heart of today's conversation about bodies is an idea that's simple in theory but complex and courageous in practice: body positivity. It's more than a buzzword or a social media hashtag. It's a movement, a philosophy, and, for many, a daily challenge.

To understand why body positivity matters now, it helps to step back and ask: What does it truly mean? The origins of body positivity lie in resistance and hope. In the late 1960s, a group called the National Association to Aid Fat Americans (now known as the National Association to Advance Fat Acceptance, or NAAFA) challenged the relentless negativity aimed at larger bodies. Members demanded the right to exist and to be treated with dignity—something many still fight for today. Their efforts soon intertwined with broader calls for equality, including the feminist movement, which began to talk loudly about the harm of rigid beauty standards.

Fast-forward to the 1990s and early 2000s: the term "body positive" found its home in grassroots communities and therapy settings. At its roots, body positivity was about giving people—especially those marginalized for their size, skin color, gender, or ability—a way to claim space and say, "My body deserves respect, too." The movement blossomed, gradually shifting from mainly speaking out against fat discrimination to a broader call for acceptance of all bodies.

In current times, body positivity is both a personal mantra and a political statement. It asks that everyone, regardless of shape, size, or difference, recognize their body as worthy of kindness. Body positivity is often misrepresented as loving every part of oneself all the time. In reality, it's more nuanced: it's about recognizing that everyone has value and dignity, even when inner and outer critics get loud. Sonya Renee Taylor, author and activist, says, "We will not go back to the failed methods of self-punishment and shame as tools for love and change." This view makes body positivity both radical and realistic, a promise and a challenge.

Yet, for all its well-meaning intentions, body positivity faces hurdles. Many people still struggle tremendously with their body image. These struggles don't always look the same. For some, it's a whisper of doubt in the dressing room. For others, it's years spent dodging the camera lens or worrying about a number on the scale. The nonprofit Mental Health America estimates that roughly one in five teens faces significant issues with their body image, and that negative self-image is linked to higher rates of depression and anxiety.

Anecdotes abound. Maya, a sixteen-year-old, remembers dreading pool parties in middle school because she wore a size few of her classmates did. "I used to fake being sick so I wouldn't have to swim," she shares. "It wasn't just the suit; it was thinking everyone would judge me." Meanwhile, James, now in college, describes constantly comparing himself to the fit athletes he scrolled past on Instagram. "It got to the point where I couldn't even go to the gym without feeling embarrassed."

Body image struggles don't always fade with time. Studies show that adults, too, grapple with self-criticism. According to the National Eating Disorder Association, about 70% of women and 43% of men report dissatisfaction with their bodies at some stage. This dissatisfaction can shape eating habits, relationships, and how individuals move through the world. Dr. Linda Bacon, an expert in weight science, puts it this way: "Body image doesn't exist in a vacuum. It's built by every message we receive—from family, community, culture—and what we choose to believe."

These messages come from many sources, but few shape them as forcefully as media and, more recently, social media. For decades, glossy magazines featured models who fit an almost impossibly narrow definition of beauty: thin but not too thin, tall, with certain skin and hair types. Television, movies, and advertising followed suit. Audiences—especially young girls—saw these images repeated over and over and learned, consciously or not, that their bodies didn't measure up.

Social media has changed the formula, but not always for the better. On one hand, the rise of platforms like Instagram, TikTok, and YouTube has allowed people to represent themselves in ways traditional media never did. Today, you can follow plus-size fashion bloggers, disabled athletes, and individuals of every skin tone, shape, and gender. Someone like Lizzo, with her bold embrace of her body and message of self-love, stands as inspiration for millions.

But there's a darker side to this digital revolution. Algorithms often reward posts showing certain bodies or lifestyles, making it seem as though those who fit a particular mold are more celebrated. Filters and photo-editing apps let users erase blemishes and reshape bodies with a few taps, giving rise to what some experts call "Snapchat Dysmorphia"—where people seek to look like their filtered selves in real life.

According to research from Common Sense Media, 35% of teenagers say they worry about their body image because of social media.

For every supportive community, there are trolls and critics eager to tear others down. Anonymous comments can hurt more than jeers in the school hallway. Even positive posts about self-love can sometimes feel overwhelming—setting an almost unattainable standard of constant confidence. As journalist Amanda Mull wrote, "Social media makes it easy to believe everyone has body confidence figured out except you."

Not everyone's experience within body positivity—or body image—looks the same. The conversation shifts, deepens, and sometimes fractures along lines of race, gender, ability, sexuality, and more. This is where intersectionality comes in, a term coined by Kimberlé Crenshaw to describe how social categories overlap, creating unique experiences of discrimination or privilege.

Take, for example, how beauty ideals often center white, thin, able-bodied individuals. People of color, especially Black women, have long faced pressure to conform to Eurocentric standards. In some cultures, lighter skin is prized over darker. The fashion and beauty worlds still struggle with representation; a 2022 report by The Fashion Spot found just 48% of models at major fashion weeks were people of color, a sign of progress but also of how far things have to go.

Gender also shapes body image in profound ways. Expectations around masculinity can push boys and men to value muscular, lean physiques, sometimes at the cost of their health. For transgender and nonbinary individuals, body image can be wrapped up in dysphoria, discrimination, and lack of representation. According to The Trevor Project, 71% of transgender and nonbinary youth reported symptoms of major depressive disorder, with body image often listed as a factor.

Ability is another piece of the puzzle that's too often ignored. People with disabilities face not only inaccessibility in spaces and products but also media narratives that either erase them or frame their bodies as objects of pity or inspiration. "People with disabilities want to be seen as whole, not as exceptions," says advocate Alice Wong, founder of the Disability Visibility Project.

Class and access play a part, too. Not everyone has the same access to nutritious food, safe places to move, or culturally relevant care. For some, the cost of gym memberships, therapy, or even a simple pair of jeans that fit is out of reach.

Recognizing these differences doesn't mean giving up on body positivity; it means making the movement stronger and more honest. It pushes everyone to ask whose voices are missing from the story and to make room for new, often uncomfortable, truths.

Given these truths, a question often arises: What does body positivity look like in real life? Is it just about acceptance, or are there practical steps people can take? Pragmatic body positivity is about more than affirmations; it's about bridging the gap between loving your body and taking care of it, between acceptance and agency.

For starters, body positivity doesn't demand that you feel ecstatic about every inch of yourself every single day. Some days, neutrality is a triumph. "Body neutrality" is a term gaining traction, focusing less on appearance and more on what bodies can do. Movement leaders like Jessamyn Stanley, a yoga teacher and author, urge people to appreciate their bodies' strength, flexibility, and resilience regardless of how they look in a mirror.

Therapists often guide clients to separate self-worth from appearance. Dr. Renee Engeln, author of Beauty Sick, encourages her patients to create "body gratitude" lists—thanking their bodies for what they allow them to do rather than how they appear to others. "Focus on function, not form," she advises.

On a broader level, pragmatic body positivity calls for changes in schools, workplaces, and communities. This includes advocating for more inclusive fashion sizing, better representation in media, accessible gyms and sports leagues, and supportive mental health care. The message is clear: people deserve a world that accommodates variety, not the impossible pursuit of sameness.

Individuals find their own paths. Jeremy, a high school teacher, organizes "mirrorless" dressing days in his class to help students focus on how clothes feel rather than fixating on their reflection. Priya, a college student, hosts workshops on cooking for pleasure and nourishment, not punishment. These small steps accumulate, creating ripples that make real difference.

Taking action also means speaking up—whether defending a friend against body shaming or calling out institutions that promote unhealthy ideals. Advocacy, both big and small, drives change. As model and activist Hunter McGrady says, "Your one brave voice can give others permission to speak."

There will always be days when the world seems determined to reduce people to a before-and-after photo or a list of supposed flaws. The promise of body positivity isn't perfection or complete invulnerability. Instead, it's in the messy, ongoing work of showing up for oneself and others—especially the most overlooked. Every candid conversation and every courageous break from the script chips away at an old story and builds the possibility of a new one.

A body, after all, is more than an image. It's a vessel for laughter, a tool for showing love, a bridge to the world. The challenge and promise of body positivity is learning to see—really see—the whole person, and not just the shape they take. Each person's journey is different. What connects them, though, is the hope that everyone can find not just peace with their bodies, but also power in them. The stories told, the truths confronted, and the kindness shared make this more than a movement—they make it a new way of living.

Chapter 2

It's a simple moment: a teenage girl stands in front of her bedroom mirror. She draws a deep breath and tugs at a strand of hair, wishing it would fall just so. Her eyes dart to her phone—one swipe reveals a world where faces are flawless and bodies sculpted perfectly, almost unreal. The urge to fit that mold feels overwhelming, as if some silent judge is watching and weighing her worth with every passing second. Though she may not realize it, this feeling doesn't happen by accident; it's shaped by something much larger: the male gaze and all the expectations that come with it.

Defining the Male Gaze: Origins and Societal Influence

The term "male gaze" may sound academic, but its meaning is woven into everyday life in the most ordinary and extraordinary places. Coined by film theorist Laura Mulvey in 1975, the phrase describes a way of looking at the world through a masculine, often heterosexual, point of view. Films, ads, and many forms of media are created as if men are the main audience. Women, in these scenarios, are portrayed less as individuals with their own stories and more as objects—meant to attract, to please, and to be watched.

Take a moment to recall popular movies, music videos, or even magazine covers. Who is being shown, and for whom are they being shown? Very often, female characters are introduced with slow camera pans on their bodies. Their stories may revolve around being noticed, admired, or desired. These images send subtle signals about what is valuable. Psychologist Dr. Sarah Murnen puts it this way: "If the world keeps showing women as decoration, we learn to value women for their appearance more than their ideas, dreams, or talents."

It's important to understand that the male gaze is not about hating men or accusing all men of intentional harm. Instead, it's a much deeper idea about who gets to define what's "normal" or "beautiful," and whose perspectives are considered when stories are told or images are created. This kind of gaze seeps into the stories we hear, the ads we see, and even the rules we follow at school, at work, or online. It shapes what is seen as desirable, valuable, and, above all, worthy.

Girls don't wake up wishing for smaller waists and shinier hair on their own. These thoughts are planted and watered by a culture that highlights and rewards a very specific type of beauty—often narrow, unrealistic, and deeply influenced by the preferences of men in power. According to a 2020 study by the Geena Davis Institute on Gender in Media, women are still twice as likely as men to be shown in revealing clothing in top films, and their bodies are more likely to be the focus of the camera. This repetitive exposure quietly reinforces the message: a woman's value lies mainly in how she looks.

How Media Shapes Perceptions of Beauty and Value

Scroll through any social media feed, flip through TV channels, or browse the latest magazines, and the message repeats itself with endless variations. Beauty, it seems, is one look. Thin but curvy, youthful but somehow ageless, with smooth skin, glossy hair, and picture-perfect smiles. Stylists, editors, and influencers often tweak images with lighting, filters, or digital editing, turning people into nearly impossible ideals. It's easy to begin believing these ideals are not only possible but required.

In a world with more than 95 million photos uploaded to Instagram every day (according to data from 2022), it's no wonder that images become the yardstick by which so many measure themselves. It's not just about looking a certain way; it's about performing, presenting, and perfecting. Ads for skincare, makeup, and hair products rarely focus on self-expression; instead, they promise transformation and approval. The voice is gentle but firm: Achieve this look, and you will be loved, respected, noticed.

Even when companies try to show "diversity," the idea of beauty may not really broaden that much. Studies from Dove's Self-Esteem Project found that while girls admire a wider range of looks, they are still most often praised for fitting into old patterns—being slender, having clear skin, and so on. "We have to understand what we see in media is carefully curated—it's not real," says body image researcher Dr. Renee Engeln. "The more we compare ourselves to these images, the more likely we are to feel like we're not good enough."

The problem doesn't end with images. Scripts, jokes, storylines—they all play a role. Think of how often female characters exist mainly to serve as a love interest, or how punchlines rely on shaming women for their looks. Small wonders become big anxieties. Instead of asking what makes someone joyful or unique, the question turns to: Do I match up? Am I pretty enough? In classrooms across the country, research finds that by age 13, over 50% of girls report feeling dissatisfied with how they look, influenced by what they see around them.

It may seem harmless—just entertainment, just ads—but these messages work quietly, shaping not just what people want to look like, but what they believe makes them worthy of kindness and belonging.

Internalizing the Gaze: Effects on Self-Esteem and Body Image

Little by little, the world's judgments slip under the skin. The "gaze" doesn't just stay outside; it slowly turns inward until it becomes the way girls view themselves. The scientific word for this is "self-objectification," which means picking apart your own appearance as if you were looking at yourself through someone else's, often critical, eyes.

Research by Dr. Barbara Fredrickson and Dr. Tomi-Ann Roberts shows that teens who learn to judge themselves this way—who constantly wonder how they look or whether they're measuring up—report higher rates of shame, anxiety, and even depression. When the mirror becomes a kind of silent judge, joy begins to shrink, and self-criticism flourishes.

It's not only about physical appearance. Girls begin to watch themselves in social settings, in class, and among friends. They second-guess how they sound, how they laugh, even how they sit—worried they'll be seen as "too much" or "not enough." A 2023 survey by the American Association of University Women found that over 70% of girls between ages 12 and 18 believe they need to look a certain way to be liked or accepted by peers, a belief amplified by the images and messages seen all around them.

The impacts are far-reaching. Consider the ways some girls drop out of sports, stop raising their hands in class, or withdraw from social activities—not because they lack interest, but because they fear being judged. One high-school student, Maya, recalls, "I loved swimming, but I quit the team in ninth grade. I just couldn't stand the idea of people seeing my body in a swimsuit. Suddenly it felt like my skills didn't matter if I didn't look a certain way."

These stories are common. And the inner critic can seem relentless. Dr. Engeln, in her book "Beauty Sick," writes, "If you're always worried about how you look, you don't have any space left for dreaming, creating, or being yourself." The energy spent on self-surveillance—the constant mental checking and comparing—leaves less room for learning new things, forming meaningful friendships, or pursuing talents that have nothing to do with appearance.

This isn't to say self-awareness is bad. But when awareness turns into harsh judgment, or when self-worth becomes chained to meeting someone else's imaginary standard, it's time to pause and question: Whose gaze am I living for?

Breaking the Cycle: Recognizing and Challenging External Validation

Identifying the source of these pressures is the first step in breaking their grip. It can be freeing to realize that the desire for approval is not a personality flaw; it's a response to a world that places so much value on external validation. Every like, compliment, and approving glance feels good, but it can quickly become a habit—a need to constantly check up on how others see you, rather than how you feel about yourself.

Consider Lily, a sophomore in high school, who shares, "Honestly, I started posting selfies just for fun, but after a while, I'd delete the ones that didn't get enough likes. It stopped being about liking how I looked and started being about whether other people did." Social media is designed to keep people seeking this kind of feedback. The rush of a new notification can feel like a burst of sunshine—or, when it's missing, like a cloud overhead.

Experts in adolescent psychology, like Dr. Rachel Simmons, explain that this pattern can be hard to break: "When validation comes from outside—when it's dependent on what others say about us—it's almost never enough. We start chasing it, and the chase never really ends." The risk is that real self-worth—the deep confidence that you are valuable just as you are—gets lost along the way.

But there is power in seeing the systems at play. When people start to spot the pattern—how ads, shows, and comments push them to care so much about seeing themselves through someone else's lens—they begin to reclaim some control. It's not always easy, and it takes practice, but recognizing the source can turn anxiety into curiosity. Why do I want this? Who benefits if I feel insecure? What do I value, truly, for myself?

Small moments of resistance add up. It might mean keeping certain apps off your phone, unfollowing accounts that make you feel small, or surrounding yourself with people who lift you up for reasons that go beyond skin deep. When girls and women come together to talk honestly about these experiences—to laugh, question, and share what's real—something cracks open. There's a relief in saying, "It doesn't have to be like this."

Making these shifts is not about ignoring compliments or pretending the urge to fit in doesn't exist. It's about putting those urges in their place—letting them be just one voice among many, rather than the main driver of self-worth. As poet and feminist Audre Lorde wrote, "If I didn't define myself for myself, I would be crunched into other people's fantasies for me and eaten alive."

Practical Steps for Cultivating Self-Worth from Within

Healing from the effects of the male gaze and building self-worth from the inside is a journey, one that unfolds slowly. Still, there are practical steps—small, powerful choices—that build real confidence over time and shift focus away from the mirror and the opinions of others.

Start by getting curious about your own inner voice. When you catch yourself judging your appearance in the way social media might, pause. Ask: "Who am I trying to please?" Sometimes, simply noticing the thought is enough to break its spell. Dr. Kristin Neff, an expert on self-compassion, teaches that kindness toward ourselves is crucial: "When we treat ourselves with the same care we offer friends, we begin to see that our value does not depend on external approval."

Another practice is to make a list—not of things you like about how you look, but of things you like about who you are. Are you creative? Loyal? Funny? Brave? Focus on the qualities that can't be captured in a photo. One group of middle school girls, after making such lists, found that their answers were all different and personal. Some said, "I'm patient with animals," or "I'm a good listener." Seeing these qualities in black and white helped them remember what really matters.

Expanding your role models can help, too. Seek out stories of people who challenge what society says is beautiful or valuable. Authors like Roxane Gay and Michaela Cole have written honestly about loving themselves despite pressures to conform, and their journeys offer inspiration and practical tips. Diverse stories remind us that there are so many ways to be smart, strong, and beautiful. Each example becomes a little crack in the old, rigid mold.

It's also important to build relationships that support true self-worth. Surround yourself with people who appreciate your ideas, humor, and dreams—not just those who dwell on the surface. Support each other in calling out negative self-talk or unrealistic expectations, whether they come from outside or from within. In groups, friends can challenge each other to notice the messages in media or to talk openly about insecurities, making those worries much less powerful.

Daily habits matter, too. Try to limit the time spent comparing, especially on social media. If you notice certain accounts leave you feeling worse, unfollow them. Replace them with pages that show a wider variety of bodies, talents, and expressions. Consider journaling about small victories—not just grades or appearance, but moments you felt proud, learned something, or helped someone else.

Don't forget to celebrate what your body can do, rather than just how it looks. Whether it's walking, dancing, playing an instrument, or laughing until your sides hurt, every person's body carries them through moments of joy and challenge. Focusing on gratitude for what your body helps you achieve can shift attention away from its appearance and toward its amazing abilities.

Some girls find that learning a new skill, volunteering, or exploring a new interest helps build confidence from the inside out. When your mind is covered in paint from an art project or you're laughing with friends after a sports game, thoughts of perfection tend to fade into the background.

Finally, it's okay to talk about times when you feel anxious or insecure. Trusted adults, counselors, or friends can often offer reminders and support. Even experts feel this pressure sometimes—Dr. Renee Engeln shares, "None of us are immune. But talking about it is the first step toward making it smaller, less powerful."

As you think about mirrors, likes, and comments, remember this isn't a solo journey. Changing the way you see yourself—and the world—takes time, honesty, and courage, but every step counts.

Changing how we value ourselves rarely happens overnight. It's built through thousands of choices—to pause, notice, and care for ourselves just a little more gently. When we learn to see through the gaze that matters most—our own—we open up space for new dreams, deeper belonging, and a confidence that can't be measured or diminished by a passing glance. Each time you choose to trust your own value, you build a future where you get to define for yourself what makes you whole and worthy. The mirror becomes just a reflection—never the judge.

Chapter 3

Imagine stepping onto a stage, your heart pounding as dozens of eyes settle on you. Maybe you're about to sing, or give a speech, or walk onto the field as the crowd cheers. In these moments, the wave of excitement isn't just about what you're about to do. It's also about how others will respond. Will they clap? Will they smile, nod their heads, raise their voices in support? Deep down, almost everyone craves those reactions—some sign from the world that what we're doing matters.

But imagine another scenario, where the applause is gone, and it's just you alone in your room. You hum the song again, or reread the lines of your speech, or toss a ball against the wall just to feel its weight. Nobody is there to see you, to praise you, or to judge you. In that quiet, whose opinion matters most? The line between external validation and internal self-worth rests quietly in those empty, silent spaces.

Distinguishing External Validation from Internal Self-Worth

Long before social media, people cared about what

others thought of them. Evolutionary psychologists say it's in our nature. Acceptance used to mean survival—being part of the group meant shelter, food, protection. Dr. Kristin Neff, a leading voice in self-compassion research, explains: "Validation from others activates the reward centers of our brains." It feels good, even today, when someone says, "Great job!" or "You look wonderful!"

But let's take a closer look. External validation is like a spotlight. It shines bright, but only while it's pointed at you. Cheers fade, compliments end, and you're left waiting for the next beam of approval. Internal self-worth, on the other hand, is like a lantern you hold within. Its steady glow comes from your own sense of value, regardless of applause, opinions, or Instagram likes.

When you rely only on external validation, your confidence is borrowed. It dances at the mercy of the crowd, their moods or distractions. When it comes from within, your self-worth stands taller, steadier—it isn't shaken by anyone else's silence or disapproval.

Separating the two isn't always easy. Think of Ava, a high school student who brings home report cards decorated with "A's." Her parents beam with pride, telling her, "You're so smart!" For a while, Ava feels unstoppable. But one semester gets tough—and when the grades dip, so does her spirit. Her confidence, it turns out, was as fragile as the next test.

Contrast Ava with Jordan, who smiles quietly to himself after a long week of studying. He doesn't broadcast his grades or seek out praise. Instead, his pride comes from knowing he did his best, regardless of the outcome. Jordan's self-worth isn't rooted in anyone's reaction—it's planted firmly within.

Recognizing Healthy vs. Unhealthy Validation-Seeking

Let's be clear: wanting recognition isn't bad. We all need encouragement. In fact, healthy validation can give us a boost, help us gauge where we are, and motivate us to keep going. The coach who says, "Great hustle out there!" or the friend who cheers, "You've got this!"—that's fuel for the journey, not the sole source of our energy.

However, something shifts when validation becomes a need rather than a bonus. That shift is subtle, but unmistakable. Dr. Guy Winch, a psychologist known for his work on emotional health, points to "validation addiction"—when people depend on others' approval and feel empty without it. This dependence can creep up on anyone.

Picture Maya, who scrolls through her phone late at night to check her latest post. A single heart or a thumbs up gives her a buzz, but an hour later, she's restless again. Did someone comment? Is her selfie good enough? Each refresh brings a tiny high, but also a deepening hunger.

This cycle isn't limited to social media. Some people maintain friendships out of fear of being left out, constantly shape their words to fit a mold, or hesitate to try new things, worried about disapproval. It can feel like walking a tightrope, balancing every move for the next round of applause.

Unhealthy validation-seeking shapes us in harmful ways. It can lead to anxiety, depression, and a loss of personal identity. When the approval stops, what's left? The emptiness can be sharper than any criticism. Even when the praise rolls in, it's never enough—just a sip of water in a thirst that never truly goes away.

Healthy validation, in contrast, feels quieter. It's a high five after a team effort. It's reflecting with someone you trust, genuinely listening to their encouragement, and then using it as a checkpoint rather than a lifeline. You feel grateful, but not dependent. It uplifts, but doesn't define.

Shifting from Approval-Seeking to Self-Affirmation

Transitioning from chasing approval to cultivating self-affirmation doesn't happen overnight. It's a gradual, deliberate shift—more like gently turning a ship than flipping a switch. At the heart of self-affirmation is a simple idea: you matter, just as you are, regardless of who claps or doesn't.

Self-affirmation isn't about ignoring feedback or living

in isolation. It means listening to others, but also weighing their opinions against your own values and goals. Dr. Carol Dweck, famous for her work on growth mindset, reminds students: "Don't let praise undermine your ability to take risks." In other words, if applause is your only goal, you'll stay on safe ground—never truly exploring your own limits.

Consider Ethan, a middle schooler who realizes he keeps signing up for clubs his friends like, not what interests him. He feels torn—if he drops out, will they think less of him? One afternoon, he signs up for chess club, simply because he enjoys puzzles. The first few weeks are awkward; he misses the familiar faces. But as he improves and begins to win matches, Ethan feels a pride that didn't hinge on anyone watching.

Self-affirmation starts with honesty, not bravado. It's taking note of your strengths and also your struggles. It's telling yourself, "I tried, I grew, I showed up—no matter what others think." Over time, affirming your own efforts and values crafts a sturdier type of confidence. This confidence is far less likely to collapse under the pressure of criticism or indifference.

Practical self-affirmation can take many forms. Some people write daily reminders of what they appreciate about themselves. Others set small, achievable goals, recognize their efforts, and accept compliments without fishing for more. Self-affirmation is the gentle voice that says, "I'm enough," even on days when it feels hardest to believe.

Building Lasting Confidence Through Personal Achievements

Each person's confidence is built on a collection of moments—big victories, quiet efforts, memorable failures, and new beginnings. Lasting confidence doesn't just happen because someone calls you "talented" or "smart." It grows when you set out to do something hard, work for it, and discover what you're capable of—even if nobody else is looking.

In 2018, a group of researchers at the University of Illinois found that students who tied confidence to their own progress, rather than external praise, showed higher levels of grit and satisfaction. They didn't just feel better—they performed better over time, facing setbacks with determination instead of collapse.

Personal achievement is about much more than trophies or report cards. It's the feeling you get after finishing a book you didn't think you could read, or finally nailing that skateboard trick after a hundred falls. These small moments accumulate, slowly thickening the roots of your inner confidence.

Take Sofia, who decided to learn guitar. At first, her fingers ached, and the songs sounded clumsy. She wanted her parents to notice, to tell her she was a natural. When they didn't, she nearly gave up. But something kept her going—a desire to master just one song. Weeks passed. She could finally strum the melody, smooth and steady. That moment, alone in her room, felt bigger than any applause she could imagine.

This is the heart of internal confidence. It's built, brick by brick, through efforts that matter to you. Sometimes you'll have cheerleaders. Sometimes you'll have critics. But the most important voice belongs to you, whispering, "Keep going. I see what you've done."

Looking back, adults often realize their proudest achievements weren't the ones that won awards, but the ones they accomplished when nobody was watching. The marathon finished alone. The art project no one saw. The kindness that wasn't posted online.

Lasting confidence flourishes when it isn't dependent on immediate results. Confidence is holding onto effort, not just accomplishment. This mindset not only makes you stronger—it makes you braver. Because when your self-worth is anchored in your own journey, risk and failure cease being threats. They become part of the story.

Practical Exercises for Fostering Internal Confidence

So how do you kindle that steady inner flame? There are concrete, every day practices—small but mighty steps—that help grow internal confidence, regardless of what the world throws at you.

Begin with a daily self-check-in. Each evening, take five minutes to reflect on your day. Ask yourself, "What did I do today that took effort?" Write down even the smallest things—a difficult conversation you finally started, a math problem you worked at for an hour, a joke you told that made someone smile. Dr. Martin Seligman, often called the founder of positive psychology, recommends this exercise to help people focus on effort instead of outcome, which boosts resilience.

Another valuable technique is the "Compliment Jar." Every time you recognize something positive about yourself—your bravery, kindness, persistence—write it on a slip of paper and drop it into a jar. On tough days, reach in and read a few. These reminders are like notes from your inner coach, quiet proof of your strengths and progress.

Visualization plays a powerful role, too. Before tackling a challenge, close your eyes and imagine yourself succeeding. Feel the nerves, then picture yourself steadying them. The soccer player who imagines making a goal is more likely to score than the one plagued by doubt; studies show that rehearsal in the mind shapes confidence in real life.

It's equally important to reframe mistakes and setbacks. When something goes wrong, pause and ask: "What did I learn? What can I try differently next time?" Lao Tzu, the ancient philosopher, wrote, "He who gains a victory over other men is strong; but he who gains a victory over himself is all powerful." Each time you learn from a setback, your self-worth thickens.

Try surrounding yourself with people who support, rather than rescue, you. Healthy encouragement means someone believes in your ability and respects your journey, rather than solving problems for you or smothering you in praise. Seek out coaches, teachers, or friends who ask, "What's your next step?" rather than doling out compliments just to make you feel better.

Finally, practice self-compassion. If your inner critic replays every mistake, counter it with the steady voice that says, "It's okay to stumble. I am still learning." Dr. Neff insists, "Self-compassion is not self-indulgence. It is care, for ourselves, as we would care for a friend." Writing a letter to yourself, as to a friend who's struggling, can help anchor your inner confidence in empathy and truth.

Each of these exercises shines a light on your own efforts, celebrating growth over perfection. Over time, they rebuild your relationship with yourself, making external validation a bonus, not a necessity.

The journey from needing approval to appreciating your own achievements is never entirely finished. Each day, life will offer new chances to measure your worth, to compare yourself to others, and to wonder if you're enough. You might glance up, searching for a sign from someone else, but then, in the quiet space between moments, you'll remember: your most meaningful applause is the kind you give yourself.

This is where lasting confidence is born—not in the glow of a spotlight, but in the steady warmth that remains when the world turns quiet and you see, clearly, what you're truly capable of.

Chapter 4

Have you ever caught yourself whispering unkind words in your own ear? It's something almost everyone does, sometimes without even realizing it. Those little phrases—"I'm not good enough," "I always mess things up," "No one will like me"—can sneak into your thoughts and hang around like unwelcome guests. Yet, as simple as words may seem, the conversations you have with yourself have a powerful pull on your mood, your confidence, and even the choices you make every day. Let's pull back the curtain and shine a gentle light on the internal stories you tell yourself, how they take shape, and how you can transform them into something supportive, sturdy, and sincerely your own.

Understanding Your Current Inner Narrative: Identifying Patterns in Self-Talk

Most people don't remember the first time they told themselves they couldn't do something. Maybe it was the echo of a teacher's disapproval after a test, or the disappointment in your parent's eyes when you brought home a scraped knee and a ripped shirt. No matter when it started, these moments can settle quietly into the back of your mind and take root.

Start by slowing down and simply listening to your own thoughts. What's the background noise in your mind? Are your inner words cheering you on, or are they dragging you down?

Jenna, for example, noticed she spent her afternoons thinking, "I'll never get caught up," whenever her homework piled up. At first, she thought this was just the truth. After all, there were so many assignments. But once she started writing down her thoughts, she realized, "I actually get a lot done—I just don't notice it because I'm too busy telling myself I'm falling behind."

It's helpful to notice not just the words you use with yourself, but when you use them. Do negative thoughts swarm when you're tired, hungry, or stressed? Do you judge yourself more harshly after a mistake, or when comparing yourself to someone else? Keeping a "self-talk log" for a week—just jot notes in your phone or a notebook—can reveal surprising patterns.

Dr. Kristin Neff, a leading researcher on self-compassion, notes, "Much of what we say to ourselves, we would never dream of saying to a friend." That contrast is an important clue. If what you're telling yourself isn't as kind or fair as what you'd offer a friend, it may not be your true voice—it might be an old echo you've outgrown.

The Science Behind Self-Talk: How Words Shape Beliefs and Behaviors

So why does self-talk matter so much? Science gives us some fascinating answers. Thoughts trigger emotions, which in turn influence our actions. If your mind is full of defeatist predictions—"I can't do this," "People will laugh at me"—your body reacts with stress, worry, or hesitation. Over time, this isn't just a feeling: it becomes a habit.

Cognitive scientist Dr. Ethan Kross has shown that self-talk acts like a coach on your shoulder—or sometimes, a heckler. In experiments, students who used supportive, encouraging self-talk before public speaking felt less nervous and performed better. It's more than pep-talk; it's brain chemistry. When you think positive, self-affirming thoughts, your brain releases chemicals like dopamine and serotonin, boosting your motivation and sense of well-being.

Negative self-talk, on the other hand, can light up the same areas of the brain as physical pain. That's partly why harsh words—even if you whisper them to yourself—can feel so uncomfortable. Harvard researcher Dr. Daniel Goleman describes the brain's negativity bias: "Your mind is like Velcro for the bad stuff and Teflon for the good." So negative messages stick, while positive ones slip away unless you give them extra attention.

The good news is that your brain is wired to change. Neuroplasticity means your mental habits can reshape themselves over time. With practice, you can teach your mind to change its tune, replacing the old script with a narrative that helps you thrive. As Dr. Carol Dweck, the psychologist known for her work on growth mindset, puts it: "Becoming is better than being." What you say to yourself shapes not just how you feel now, but who you'll become tomorrow.

Uncovering Negative Self-Talk: Recognizing and Challenging Inner Criticisms

So how do you catch that sneaky, unhelpful voice? Sometimes it's obvious—like a bully blurting out, "You're not smart enough." Other times, it's sly and quiet, blending into the rhythm of your thoughts so well you don't notice.

Start by watching for a few common patterns. Do you spot any absolutes creeping in, like "always" or "never"? For example: "I always mess up," or "I'll never get this right." Absolutes are rarely true, but they make mistakes feel permanent.

Watch for comparisons, too. "He's better than me at everything." "She never makes mistakes." These thoughts crop up most often when you're scrolling through social media or listening to other people's accomplishments. Remember, what people share is usually their highlight reel, not their struggles.

Another signal is catastrophizing—jumping to the worst-case scenario. Maybe you trip over your words in class, and instantly think, "Now everyone will think I'm dumb forever." Catching that leap is the first step to reining it in.

Ali, a high school freshman, fought with stage fright all semester. He'd tell himself, "I'm going to mess up, and they'll all laugh." But when he challenged that with, "Really? Has anyone ever laughed before?" he realized the answer was no. In fact, most people were nervous, too. The fear wasn't based in reality but in an old tape playing in his head.

Journaling can be a powerful way to slow your thoughts and question them. Write out your worries, then ask yourself: "Is this fact or fear? What would I say to a friend who thought this?" Sometimes, bringing your inner critic out into the daylight takes away its bite.

Techniques for Rewriting Your Narrative: Transforming Self-Talk into Empowerment

Catching negative self-talk is important, but what comes next? This is where you actively take control, guiding your thoughts like a gardener tending to new shoots. Every time you swap a critical phrase for a compassionate one, you strengthen positive pathways in your brain.

One effective tool is reframing. Rather than, "I can't do

this," try, "This is new for me, so it's okay to not get it right away." Instead of, "I always fail," try, "I didn't succeed this time, but what can I learn for next time?" The key is to get specific. Vague positives like, "I'm great," can feel untrue when you're struggling. But concrete, encouraging thoughts—"I prepared as best as I could"—feel believable.

Affirmations, used well, are another powerful technique. Write sentences like, "I am learning every day," or "Mistakes are part of growing." Some people find it helpful to say them out loud in the mirror or keep them as phone reminders. Researchers at Carnegie Mellon found that students who practiced positive self-affirmations before stressful exams felt calmer and performed better. Their inner narratives weren't just wishful thinking; they shaped their confidence and results.

Cognitive Behavioral Therapy (CBT) teaches a method called "disputation"—challenging the truth of harsh automatic thoughts. If your mind says, "I'll always be alone," look for real evidence. Are there people who care about you? Are there times you've made new friends? By questioning exaggerations, you open up space for a fairer perspective.

You don't have to flood your mind with relentless positivity. Instead, aim for honesty and gentleness. "I made a mistake" can be paired with "That doesn't mean I'm a failure." When you stumble, remind yourself: setbacks are not proof of your inadequacy.

As Dr. Brené Brown writes, "Talk to yourself like you would to someone you love."

Visualization is another method to reshape self-talk. Before a big event, close your eyes and picture yourself handling it with determination, even if you're nervous. Imagine your inner voice saying, "You can handle this," or "Whatever happens, you will figure it out." Athletes, musicians, and public speakers often use visualization to build confidence and calm nerves before big moments.

Some people create "confidence anchors"—small objects or phrases that remind them of their strengths. Nadia, a young artist, wore a bracelet her grandmother gave her and touched it whenever she doubted herself. It was a friendly nudge to remember her own resilience when doubt crept in.

Sustaining Change: Making Positive Self-Talk a Daily Habit

You wouldn't expect to play an instrument perfectly the first time you pick it up. Rewriting your self-talk is just as much a practice, not a one-time project. Like watering a plant, small, steady actions make the biggest difference over time.

Setting reminders in your environment helps tremendously. Stick encouraging notes on your mirror, leave a positive message as your phone background, or join a friend in sharing one thing you did well each day. These small cues steadily build new habits.

Some people benefit from structured routines, such as starting each morning with three positive intentions, or ending the day by writing down one thing they're grateful for. These practices shift attention away from criticism and towards growth.

It's also important to show patience. There will be days when the old narrative tries to slip back in—perhaps when you're tired, stressed, or things don't go as planned. Recognize these moments as normal. One harsh thought doesn't erase your progress; it's just a sign to check in with yourself and offer a bit more kindness.

When setbacks happen, remember the story of Maya Angelou, the poet and memoirist. She once said, "We may encounter many defeats but we must not be defeated." Her life was filled with challenges, but she kept rewriting her own narrative, turning pain into poetry and hope. Your own story isn't fixed—it bends with each word you choose.

Over time, you'll notice your new inner voice showing up without as much effort. "I've handled tough things before; I can do this." Or, "It's okay to need help." This shift might feel slow, but it's sure. Researchers at the University of California found that students who practiced self-compassion and positive self-talk showed better resilience during exams and stress.

The journey of rewriting your inner conversation isn't about banishing vulnerability or pretending nothing hurts; it's about building a kinder partnership with yourself. Each moment you offer yourself understanding instead of rebuke, support instead of scorn, you lay another stone on the path toward genuine confidence.

Soften the edges of your self-judgments. Tune in to the quiet strength of encouraging words. With time, your story becomes one of growth, patience, and possibilities—carried not by perfection, but by the steady companionship of your own best voice.

Chapter 5

Human relationships have always carried an air of mystery, especially when it comes to attention—who gives it, why, and what it means. For many, figuring out why a guy looks your way, strikes up a conversation, or lingers a little longer in a room can spark flutters of curiosity and, sometimes, confusion. Unpacking male attention isn't just about satisfying curiosity, though. Understanding the different layers, motives, and tactics behind it can illuminate how we connect with each other, how feelings blossom, and why misinterpretations occur so easily.

Before we go deeper, imagine walking down a hallway at school. Sometimes a guy smiles as you pass, or maybe helps you pick up your dropped books without much fanfare. Other times, someone might offer a compliment or nervously ask for your number. Each of these moments carries its own meaning—sometimes they're not about romance at all, while other times, there's a blush just beneath the surface.

Categories of Male Attention: From Friendly to Romantic to Superficial

Male attention isn't a one-size-fits-all experience. At first glance, it might seem like every look or word means the same thing, but with a little observation, the differences become clear. Experts like Dr. John Gottman, a renowned psychologist who has studied relationships for decades, often remind us that intention matters just as much as action.

Consider the friendly type. Friendly attention is perhaps the most foundational—it's about connection without an agenda. This could be a fleeting high-five, a quick check-in about how your day is going, or simply sharing a funny story. In many groups, guys show friendship by including others in their jokes, games, or casual conversations. A lot of people mistake this for flirtation, especially if the friendliness feels enthusiastic, but most of the time, there's no romantic spark attached.

Romantic attention, on the other hand, is infused with extra energy. The guy who stammers while asking you to a movie? That's often a sign of romantic interest. This version of attention might be more tender, and sometimes more awkward—like a sudden quietness, a shy grin, or a bashful attempt at sharing something deeply personal. Researchers have found that gestures like these—direct eye contact, finding ways to spend time together, or making small sacrifices—are classic markers of budding romantic feelings.

Then, there's superficial attention. This one's often the

most visible, and sometimes, the most misleading. A compliment on appearance, a pointed glance, or playful teasing might seem flattering, but sometimes, it doesn't go deeper than surface-level. Superficial attention can be fleeting or self-serving, sometimes rooted in a desire to feel popular, validated, or simply entertained. Lisa Wade, PhD, sociologist and author of "American Hookup," notes that this type of attention often gets confused for real affection, especially in settings where social status is at play.

It's helpful to remember that these categories can overlap. A guy might begin by being friendly and, over time, feel drawn romantically. Or someone may act superficially out of bravado or inexperience, later revealing a genuine desire for connection. Everyone is learning, after all, and signals can blur.

What Triggers Male Interest: Psychological, Social, and Biological Factors

The question of what makes a guy pay special attention to someone isn't just about who walks by in the hallway or who sits in the next row. There are deeper forces at work—some rooted in the wiring of the brain, others shaped by family, community, or even pop culture.

Biologically, attraction is partly about chemistry. Human beings are wired to notice certain qualities in each other: a friendly smile, confident posture, or shared laughter. Researchers at Northwestern

University once found that people notice not just how someone looks but how they make them feel. Hormones like dopamine and adrenaline get released when we're excited or intrigued, making someone's presence light up our minds like a sparkler at night.

Psychologically, connection goes beyond looks. A boy might be drawn in by shared interests—a love for the same music, a passion for soccer, or an eagerness to tackle group projects together. Being around someone who "gets you" is comforting and thrilling. Social psychologists say that similarity is one of the strongest predictors of interest and attraction.

Socially, context matters. Sometimes boys feel pressure to show attention a certain way because that's what friends expect. If the group cheers on a dare or encourages a compliment, a guy might act bolder than he feels. Family dynamics play a role too; if someone is raised in a home where emotions are open and expressed freely, they may offer attention more confidently. Alternatively, someone who grew up with lots of teasing or guardedness might act more reserved or sarcastic.

Peer influence is powerful. Dr. Niobe Way, author of "Deep Secrets: Boys' Friendships and the Crisis of Connection," found that boys often wrestle with vulnerability because of social expectations. They might hesitate to show genuine interest for fear of being labeled "soft" or mocked by others. This tension shapes how male attention appears on the surface—

sometimes cloaked in humor, sometimes masked entirely.

Media and celebrity culture have their effects too. The movies and shows teens watch teach certain scripts about how guys are "supposed" to act: cool, detached, confident, always in control. But behind the scenes, actual emotions can be messy, hesitant, and far more sincere.

Decoding Subtle Versus Overt Signals of Male Attention

Deciphering male attention often feels like trying to read a language that changes depending on who's speaking. Some guys announce their feelings with a megaphone—think grand gestures, bold declarations, or relentless texting. Others, though, communicate through micro-moments: a glance held a beat too long, a seat saved in the lunchroom, a sudden jump to help with a heavy backpack.

Subtle signals are everywhere. Stanford psychologist Dr. Nalini Ambady, known for her groundbreaking work on "thin-slicing", found that people quickly judge intent from brief interactions. In other words, our brains are wired to pick up on the smallest cues—sometimes subconsciously. For instance, a guy might lean forward during a conversation, unconsciously wanting to be closer. If his feet are pointed toward you, it's often a sign that his attention—and maybe more—are focused on you, even if he's not aware of it himself.

Physical cues are just one piece. Listen for changes in voice; nervousness might mean his tone gets higher or he stumbles over words. Notice how he interacts when others are around. Some guys only seem extra talkative or attentive in group settings, where they feel safer, while others save their most careful attention for quiet, one-on-one moments.

Overt signals, by contrast, are hard to miss. A well-timed compliment, an invitation to hang out, or a direct question about feelings all speak clearly. There's an old saying, "fortune favors the bold," and for some guys, being clear—and maybe even a little dramatic—is their way to break the ice. Think of the promposals that take over social media each spring, or the friend who writes a song or poem as a show of affection.

But overt doesn't always mean serious. Some people act big to cover nerves or to satisfy an audience. Subtle signs can sometimes reveal truer intent, though they're easier to miss. As Dr. Ambady's research shows, trust your instincts. Often, your gut picks up on sincerity before your mind can name it.

Misread cues are common, especially when communication styles differ. One memorable example comes from a college sophomore who shared, "I thought he was just being nice when he texted me every night about homework. Turns out, he liked me and was waiting for me to notice." Missing the mark isn't a failure—it's part of learning to understand each other.

Emotional Reactions: How Men Feel and Express Interest

The myth that boys and young men are unfeeling or stoic runs deep. Yet, when the surface is scratched, a complex world of emotions emerges—sometimes clumsy, sometimes overwhelming, sometimes surprising even to themselves.

When a guy feels attracted to someone, he might experience a surge of excitement—a physical buzz, sweaty palms, or butterflies. According to Dr. Leonard Sax, expert on adolescent development, these reactions are natural responses to what's new and unknown. "The thrill of early attraction can be startling, even confusing, especially for boys taught to keep their emotions private," he explains.

Inside, there may be a swirl of self-doubt. Does she notice me? Am I being too obvious? Do I look ridiculous? For many, there's a fear of rejection sitting just beneath the smile or confidence. Social and family pressures sometimes complicate these feelings. If there's a belief that "real men don't show emotions," expressing interest might come in sideways—through teasing, sarcasm, or aloofness.

Others express interest openly and warmly. They

might take risks: giving heartfelt compliments, sharing vulnerabilities, or offering small but meaningful gifts. "We see that when boys feel safe, they express tenderness in beautiful, authentic ways," says Dr. Niobe Way. This safety—emotional and social—plays a massive role. A guy surrounded by accepting friends, or who has seen emotional openness modeled by others, is more likely to be gentle, direct, and honest in his attention.

Rejection, of course, brings its own emotional storm. Disappointment, embarrassment, and even anger can arise, though these feelings are rarely shown directly. Instead, some might withdraw, throw themselves into hobbies, or act as if nothing happened at all. A high school junior shared, "After I got turned down, I stopped talking about it. But inside, I just felt embarrassed for weeks."

Boys' friendships can offer much-needed support. Many guys talk with their friends—sometimes in code, sometimes directly—about crushes, fears, and hopes. These conversations, though brief, often provide a crucial space for sorting through feelings. When male attention is encouraged and welcomed (even if it's not returned romantically), it helps build confidence and emotional resilience.

Myths and Misunderstandings: Common Misinterpretations of Male Signals

Because attention is so loaded with possibility, it is

also easy to misunderstand. The gap between what was meant and what gets received can be vast, especially when everyone is still learning how to express and interpret signals.

One common myth is that all male attention is romantic. Simply put, not every compliment or kind word carries hidden meaning. Sometimes, a guy really is being nice out of friendliness, habit, or respect. Mistaking these moments for deeper interest can lead to awkwardness or confusion.

Pop culture hasn't helped matters, often painting every action as either obviously flirtatious or cold. But as psychologist Dr. Lisa Damour puts it, "People's actions are more layered. Often, even they don't know what they want or are feeling." It's important to look for patterns: consistent attention, conversations that seem to linger, or genuine curiosity about your life are usually stronger indicators than a single comment or shared laugh.

Another frequent misunderstanding is the belief that teasing or mocking is always a sign of affection. Sure, playful banter is common among boys, especially when they're unsure how to express themselves. But not all teasing is friendly—a boundary exists. True affection feels safe, never cruel.

There's also the stereotype of the "player," a boy who shows attention to many at once with no real intent. While some people do seek validation through multiple connections, painting all boys with this brush can be unfair and discouraging. As Dr. Gottman reminds us, most young men are sorting through complex emotions and are looking for closeness just as much as their peers.

Being clear and communicative is an antidote to misunderstanding. If a signal feels confusing, it's okay to ask questions or talk frankly. Many friendships and relationships have been saved—and made stronger—when someone found the courage to ask, "Did you mean that the way I think you did?"

The challenge, then, is to meet attention with curiosity and honesty, allowing room for both mistakes and surprises. Male attention, in all its forms, is not a code meant to be cracked once and for all, but rather a conversation and a connection in constant motion.

Learning how to read these signals, and understanding the stories behind them, is a skill that deepens both friendships and crushes. In the end, every moment of attention—no matter how clumsy or skillful—carries an invitation: to see each other more clearly, and to answer with kindness.

Chapter 6

Criticism stings. Sometimes it feels like an unexpected splash of cold water—surprising, uncomfortable, impossible to ignore. As we move through life, sharing our ideas, showing our talents, and simply being ourselves, negative attention can pop up in the most unpredictable places. Handling this attention with grace and understanding is one of the most valuable life skills you can develop—not just for your peace of mind, but for your relationships and sense of self.

Why do people criticize? Is every sharp word meant to hurt? Or is criticism sometimes a clumsy form of caring, or even a hidden opportunity? To really grow, it helps to pause and examine the complex world of criticism, both its intentions and its impact.

Understanding the Nature of Criticism—Intentions Versus Impact

Imagine showing your best friend a project you've worked on for weeks—maybe it's a drawing, a story, or your performance in a video game. Their face crumples slightly. "It's okay, but wouldn't it be better if you made the colors brighter?" Suddenly, your excitement fizzles into embarrassment. Hearing something you weren't expecting, especially from someone you trust, can mess with your emotions.

Not all criticism is created equal. According to renowned psychologist Dr. Carol Dweck, "Criticism given with the intention to help you improve can be the foundation for growth, if received with an open mind." Sometimes, criticism comes from a place of care or desire for your success. Your teacher's feedback on your essay, a friend suggesting a different way to solve a problem, even a parent setting boundaries they think are best for you—these moments, meant positively, might still land with a harsh thud in your heart.

On the other hand, some criticism is genuinely negative. This might come from jealousy, insecurity, or thoughtlessness. Maybe it's a mean comment on social media, or a classmate making fun of the way you dress. Their intention isn't to help; it's to hurt or to boost themselves at your expense.

But regardless of intention, impact is what we feel right away—fear, anger, shame, or maybe just confusion. Dr. Brené Brown, a leading expert on vulnerability, says, "We are hardwired for connection, but shame and criticism disconnect us from others and ourselves." Recognizing this difference matters: understanding that what you feel immediately is about the impact, not always the critic's intent, can help you step back before reacting.

Ask yourself: was the person trying to help, even awkwardly, or were they being unkind? Did they intend to criticize, or did their words just clumsily miss the mark? Separating someone's intention from how their words made you feel is the first step toward handling criticism with maturity.

Emotional Self-Regulation in the Face of Negative Attention

It's natural to feel a surge of feelings the moment someone criticizes you—especially if it happens in front of others, or comes from someone whose opinions you care about. Our bodies might respond before our brains can catch up. Maybe your cheeks burn, your hands get sweaty, or your heart pounds in your chest.

This is your "fight or flight" system doing its job. According to Dr. Daniel Goleman, author of Emotional Intelligence, this ancient wiring is designed to protect us from threat. Unfortunately, it can't tell the difference between real danger and hurt feelings—so a mean comment triggers the same response as seeing a snake in the grass.

What can you do in those first uncomfortable moments? Start by pausing. Count to five in your mind, take a deep breath, and notice what's happening inside your body. Psychologist Dr. Susan

David, whose research centers on emotional agility, suggests naming the emotion out loud or in your mind: "I feel embarrassed." "I'm angry." This simple act is powerful; naming our feelings helps us get a bit of distance from them, letting the thinking part of our brain take over from our more reactive side.

Sometimes it helps to have a mantra: "This is just one person's opinion." Or, "I can choose how to respond." These short, grounding sentences can help you remember that criticism, no matter how harsh, does not change your true worth or abilities.

There's wisdom, too, in giving ourselves time. If it's possible, step away from the situation. Go get some water, take a short walk—anything that lets your feelings settle so you can consider the criticism more calmly. If you're online, resist the urge to fire off a defensive response. Close the app. Breathe.

Learning to respond rather than react is a hallmark of maturity. It's not about pretending you aren't hurt, or bottling up your emotions. It's about finding space between your feelings and your next action, so you avoid regrets and understand yourself a bit better.

Reframing Criticism: Developing Empathy for Others' Perspectives

Empathy turns criticism into something we can learn from, instead of just something we have to survive. Seeing things from the other person's perspective softens our own pain and opens the door to growth.

Reflect on a time you criticized someone else—maybe a sibling for hogging the bathroom, or a teammate for missing an easy goal. Think about what drove you in that moment. Were you frustrated? Worried? Trying, in your own way, to help? Remembering the complex emotions behind our own criticism can help us understand why others act the way they do.

Dr. Kristin Neff, a leading expert on self-compassion, puts it clearly: "Empathy for others creates space for connection, even in the midst of conflict." This doesn't mean excusing truly cruel or toxic behavior. But when you try to understand where criticism is coming from, you loosen its grip on your self-image.

Maybe your parent's critical words about your study habits are rooted in their own fears about your future. Perhaps the classmate who teases you is struggling with their own self-esteem. At times, negative comments mask someone else's insecurity—a phenomenon school counselor Amanda Gorman calls "hurt people hurting people."

When you put yourself in their shoes, the world opens up. You may even feel compassion for the critic. Empathy doesn't erase the sting of harsh words, but it does help you move past feeling personally attacked. If the criticism is constructive, empathy can reveal its hidden gift: a different perspective that helps you improve.

This shift is liberating. Instead of thinking, "They're just being mean," you might start to wonder, "What's really going on with them?" or "Is this something that could make me better?" In turn, your own self-worth feels less tied to outside opinions, and more grounded in knowing yourself.

Communicating with Compassion: How to Respond Rather Than React

How you answer criticism tells others as much about your character as your talents or achievements do. Responding with compassion isn't weakness; it's a powerful sign of inner strength.

Let's consider an example. You're in a group project at school. A teammate comments, "You should let someone else do the slide design, yours are too plain." The heat rises to your face. You want to snap back, "Well, at least I do my part!" But instead, you pause.

You could say, "Thanks for the feedback—can you tell me what you'd like to see changed?" Or, "I appreciate you sharing your thoughts. Maybe you can show me the style you're thinking of?" This turns the conversation from confrontation to collaboration. You stay open, invite specifics, and keep your dignity.

According to Dr. Marshall Rosenberg, founder of Nonviolent Communication, the best responses follow a simple path: observe, name your feeling, express your needs, and make a request if needed. For example: "I noticed you said my slides were plain. I felt a bit hurt. I want to contribute to the group's success—could you help me with ideas for improvement?"

Of course, not all criticism is constructive or kindly meant. If someone's words cross the line into bullying or personal attacks, compassion may mean excusing yourself, setting boundaries, or seeking support from a trusted adult. Tact and self-respect go hand-in-hand.

Online, where comments can be especially ruthless, experts advise a similar approach. Don't reply in anger. Sometimes, the healthiest response is not to engage at all. Cyberbullying researcher Dr. Sameer Hinduja stresses, "You do not have to accept or justify every opinion expressed. Protect your mental wellness; not every critic deserves your time."

Letting go of the need to win every argument or have the last word frees enormous energy for more positive pursuits. Responding with compassion does not mean agreeing with unfair criticism; rather, it shows you move with confidence and kindness, regardless of how others choose to behave.

Transforming Personal Growth Through Constructive Handling of Criticism

What you choose to do after criticism—after the

pause, the empathy, the response—shapes the person you become.

Many high achievers credit handling criticism as a major factor in their success. NBA legend Michael Jordan once claimed, "If you accept the expectations of others, especially negative ones, then you never will change the outcome." Jordan, cut from his high school basketball team, took criticism as a challenge and turned it into motivation. His story, echoed in fields from business to the arts, isn't unique. Most people who reach their highest potential learn to view criticism as a tool for self-improvement.

Instead of internalizing every negative comment, try asking yourself: "Is there anything in this criticism I can use to get better?" Genuine growth often comes from moments of discomfort. If the critique is fair, even partially, consider how you might adjust your approach. If it's unfair or mean-spirited, you can dismiss it—a skill that takes courage and practice.

Making a habit of reflecting (not ruminating) helps clarify what you want to take in, and what you choose to leave behind. Some people keep a "criticism journal," jotting down remarks and their responses. Reviewing it over time can reveal helpful patterns—perhaps you notice similar feedback about time management, or realize certain insults don't actually match reality.

Building this habit forms emotional toughness,

sometimes called resilience. According to leading psychologist Dr. Angela Duckworth, resilience—our "grit"—isn't just pushing through pain, but "the passion and perseverance to keep improving." When you view criticism as information, not insult, you take control of your own growth.

There's also power in asking for feedback. When you actively seek out honest input, you shift from a defensive posture to a curious one. You tell the world: "I want to get better. I want to learn." This attitude draws positive attention, mentors, and opportunities your way. Remember, feedback doesn't determine your value—but your response determines your journey.

Sometimes the most growth happens after you've turned criticism into connection. You mend bonds that were weakened by anger. You find mentors among those who once critiqued you. You start to recognize the seeds of your own wisdom—the ability to disagree without burning bridges, to stay kind when others are not, and to choose compassion over resentment.

As life moves forward, criticism will never disappear entirely. We live among people with differing opinions, expectations, and triggers—family, friends, classmates, teachers, strangers online. Perfection isn't the goal; connection and self-understanding are. What matters most isn't who fires off the next sharp comment, but how you choose to meet it—with reflection, kindness, and a devotion to your own values. The world is filled with voices. Listening with empathy and responding with compassion lets you turn even the sharpest words into stepping stones toward confidence and character.

Chapter 7

Compliments: those little packets of positive attention that flutter into our lives at unexpected moments. Some arrive with a sparkle, a quick "Nice job!" or "You look great today!" making your heart do a gentle leap. Others sweep in with the force of a summer wind—well-intended, perhaps, but so big they leave you uncertain how to respond, caught between gratitude and embarrassment. It's a funny thing: while praise is supposed to feel good, it doesn't always. Just as a cool drink can be both refreshing and overwhelming if you gulp it down too fast, compliments, for all their sweetness, sometimes leave us uneasy and off-balance.

Why is it, then, that something meant to lift us up can stir such contradictory feelings? One day, a compliment lands softly, making you stand taller and smile wider. The next, the same words make you self-conscious, as if there's a spotlight shining straight into your inner world. Understanding the complexity of praise is important—not so we run from it, but so we can meet it as ourselves, without shrinking or swelling beyond our comfort.

Understanding the Double-Edged Sword of Compliments: Why Positive Attention Can Feel Unsettling

Imagine you're wearing your favorite sweater. You know you look nice, and you feel cozy inside and out. Then, a classmate stops and says, "Wow, you look amazing today!" Suddenly, instead of just feeling happy in your sweater, you're acutely aware that eyes are on you. Maybe you beam with pride. Or maybe you tug at your sleeves, unsure where to rest your hands. Sometimes, a simple compliment can flip the whole feeling of the day.

There's a reason why. Compliments, for all their kindness, draw attention to us. That attention might feel like a warm spotlight, but it might also feel harsh and glaring, depending on your mood or personality. According to Dr. Kristin Neff, an expert in self-compassion, "Receiving praise means accepting that others are watching, evaluating, and noticing you. For some, this is encouraging. For others, it triggers self-doubt, anxiety, or fear of not being able to live up to expectations."

Research from the American Psychological Association has shown that people with low self-esteem often have a harder time accepting positive feedback. It doesn't mean they don't crave kindness—it just makes them question whether they belong in the good graces of others. Even those with a solid sense of self may feel that compliments force them into a box—suddenly defined by someone else's view, not their own.

It isn't just about self-esteem, though. Family backgrounds and cultural norms play a role too. In some families, praise is plentiful; in others, it's as rare as a snowstorm in July. If you grew up where compliments were often little "teachable moments" ("That's a beautiful drawing, but next time, try coloring inside the lines"), you might carry a quiet suspicion of any praise, fearing there's a hidden "but" lurking behind it.

Yet, compliments are not all risks and traps. When truly heartfelt, they can be a thread linking us to others' appreciation and love. The challenge is holding onto ourselves when others shine that positive light our way, so we don't lose sight of our own reflection in the brightness.

Distinguishing Between Genuine Praise and Manipulation: Reading Intentions Behind Compliments

Picture yourself at a family gathering. Your aunt leans in and says, "You're always so helpful. I don't know what we'd do without you." The tone is warm, and you feel a flutter of pride. Later, a new neighbor says, with a sly grin, "You're just too smart for your own good. Bet you finish all the chores fast, huh?" Suddenly, the praise feels heavier, almost like a trap. What's the difference between these moments?

Intent. Real compliments come from a desire to acknowledge or celebrate a quality or action, with no strings attached. Manipulative praise, however, comes dressed as a gift but hides another purpose—maybe to get you to do something, to make you feel small, or to shape your choices.

Social researcher Dr. Vanessa Bohns explains, "Compliments can sometimes be a tool for social influence, not just warmth. At times, people use kind words as currency to get what they want, or to manage how you see yourself and them." This doesn't mean we should eye every compliment with suspicion, but it is wise to listen past the words and tune into what's really being said.

So, how do you tell the difference? Start with your gut. Real compliments usually feel sincere, gentle, and unforced. They don't demand a reaction, repay a favor, or come with an implied "therefore..." Manipulative praise might feel sticky—a little too much, too insistent, or oddly specific. You might notice patterns, like always being complimented right before being asked for something, or praise that's over-the-top for a small effort.

There's also context. Is the compliment given in private, or is it a public show meant for others to hear? Sometimes, flattery is used as a shield or a lure, especially if the person rarely offers genuine encouragement at other times.

When in doubt, remember: your feelings are a signal, not a flaw. If a compliment starts a conversation in your mind that feels less about joy and more about obligation or confusion, it's okay to step back and consider why that is.

Staying Grounded: Strategies for Maintaining Authenticity Amid Positive Recognition

Learning how to stay rooted in yourself, even as external praise swirls around you, is a skill worth cultivating. If you accept every compliment at face value, you might be tempted to shape your behavior to collect more, living for others' approval instead of your own inner compass. On the other hand, rejecting all praise can shut you off from genuine connection—like closing a window because of a single chilly breeze.

Author Brené Brown, renowned for her work on vulnerability and self-worth, shares that "Letting yourself be seen and recognized, for good or ill, is an act of courage. But your value doesn't rise or fall depending on others' opinions; it's something you carry, always."

So, what does it look like to stay yourself in the midst of applause, admiration, or simple thanks? First, remember that compliments are like snapshots—they capture a moment, not the whole picture of who you are. You are bigger than anyone else's words.

Take a breath when you receive a compliment. Literally—inhale, feel your feet on the ground, and pause. This tiny break can keep you from automatically brushing off praise ("Oh, it was nothing") or inflating your ego ("I know, right?"). Instead, think of the compliment as information, not an instruction. It's a reflection of how someone else sees you, not a command to become their ideal.

Some people keep a "compliment journal." When positive feedback strikes a chord, write it down, not to chase after more, but to remind yourself on tough days that others see value in you. Over time, you'll notice patterns—what qualities do people appreciate? Which compliments ring true? Which feel awkward or forced? This self-reflection helps you stay anchored, accepting genuine praise without letting it sweep you away.

Grounding yourself doesn't mean shutting out others' appreciation. Rather, it's about hearing kind words, appreciating the sentiment, but returning gently to your own sense of self after the moment passes. Like a tree in a gentle wind—you bend, you move, but your roots keep you steady.

Setting Healthy Boundaries: Accepting Praise Without Feeling Obligated

Sometimes, compliments come wrapped with invisible strings. Maybe your friend raves about your baking, then hints at another batch of cookies. Or a teacher praises your leadership but quickly hands you another responsibility. Praise can, without anyone meaning harm, become a subtle form of pressure.

This dynamic can be especially tricky if you're a people-pleaser by nature. The urge to reciprocate, repay, or keep up the "good work" can leave you exhausted—and slowly, your sense of choice slips away. Dr. Nedra Tawwab, a licensed therapist known for her work on boundaries, offers this advice: "You can appreciate praise without absorbing the responsibility to always perform or please. Saying thank you is enough—you are not required to give more just because someone noticed your effort."

If you often find yourself trapped in cycles of obligation, practice the art of the simple response. When complimented, smile and say, "Thank you. That means a lot." No need to downplay, apologize, or launch into reasons. Resist the pull to agree to more as a way of 'earning' the praise.

Let's say someone praises your problem-solving skills and then immediately asks if you'll do their math homework. You have permission—truly—to separate the compliment from the request. "Thanks, I appreciate you noticing. I can't help with that today, but good luck!" This sort of firm, but kind, response reinforces a core truth: Your value isn't based on what you do for others, but on who you are.

Sometimes, the pressure is silent. You keep getting praised as "the reliable one," so you fear letting anyone down—even when you're tired or overwhelmed. If you catch yourself dreading positive attention because of what might follow, it's a sign to pause and check if your boundaries need a tune-up.

Remember, boundaries aren't walls for keeping people out. They're gentle fences that help you care for yourself while still connecting with others. And when it comes to praise, those fences allow you to enjoy the beauty of a compliment without being pulled into a never-ending cycle of giving.

Turning Compliments Into Connection: Responding Effectively Without Losing Yourself

At their heart, compliments are a bridge—an invitation, however brief, to share a little more of yourself with someone else. The secret is to meet praise with openness, but not surrender your sense of self at the door.

Here's the challenge: how do you respond in a way that's warm and genuine, but doesn't put you on the spot or make you feel phony? Start by recognizing that every compliment carries two things—a message about you, and a message about the person giving it. By responding thoughtfully, you honor both.

Let's use a real story. Harper, a shy eighth grader, had been working for months on their art project—a mural for the school hallway. When unveiling day came, class after class stopped to admire it. Compliments poured in. At first, Harper panicked, shrinking into their hoodie, mumbling "It's no big deal." But later, an art teacher coached them: "Let the praise sit with you a moment. You worked hard. You don't have to dismiss it." Harper started saying, "Thanks, it was a lot of work, but I really loved doing it." This simple shift changed everything. Compliments became conversations, not barriers.

One trick is using "I-statements" when responding. For example: "Thank you, I'm really proud of how it turned out," or "That means a lot to me—I enjoyed the process." You're not deflecting, nor are you fishing for more. You're using praise as an opening, not a spotlight that burns.

You can also turn the moment into a genuine connection by acknowledging the giver. If someone says, "You always know what to say," you might reply, "That's kind. I hope I can do the same for you some time." This approach keeps the energy flowing, without tipping into obligation or discomfort.

Every so often, a compliment will feel awkward, especially if it's about something you aren't sure about yourself. That's okay. Respond with honesty, not deflection. "Thanks for saying that. I'm still working on believing it myself." This not only diffuses the pressure but often invites a deeper, more authentic dialogue.

Over time, as you get more comfortable with positive feedback, you'll notice a gentle confidence building. Compliments won't send you spinning. They'll become moments to pause, appreciate, and then return to your true self, undisturbed.

The art of accepting praise is, at its heart, the art of accepting yourself. It's learning to savor kind words without needing to swallow them whole or spit them out in embarrassment. It's discovering that positive attention, handled with gentle boundaries and honest reflection, can nourish your spirit rather than scatter it.

And perhaps most importantly, it's recognizing that the person you show to the world—the one who earns those genuine compliments—is someone worth celebrating, with or without the applause.

Chapter 8

There are days when the weight of the world feels sharper against your skin. Even small mistakes echo loud, and the voice inside your head seems eager to remind you of every flaw or misstep. Sometimes, we're our own harshest judges, swinging words at ourselves that we'd never dream of using with a friend. Yet, tucked within each of us is the capacity to offer gentleness and understanding—to ourselves. Self-compassion isn't about ignoring our issues, but rather, about treating ourselves with the same kindness we'd offer someone we deeply care about.

Many people have trouble even considering self-compassion because they misunderstand what it means. For some, there's a fear that being gentle with ourselves might make us lazy, selfish, or less likely to succeed. There's a myth that we must be hard on ourselves to grow. But what if being truly caring to ourselves is the real secret to lasting change?

Understanding Self-Compassion: Breaking Down Myths and Misconceptions

Kristin Neff, one of the world's leading self-compassion researchers, often explains that self-compassion is made up of three elements: self-kindness, common humanity, and mindfulness. It isn't about self-pity or wallowing in mistakes. Nor is it a self-indulgent excuse to avoid responsibility. Rather, it's a brave stance—to face our suffering with honesty, warmth, and a desire to help ourselves through it.

One major myth is that self-compassion means letting ourselves off the hook. Neff's research, however, paints the opposite picture. People who practice self-compassion are actually *more* likely to take responsibility and improve after setbacks, precisely because they don't feel crushed by shame. They see mistakes as part of learning, not as proof of unworthiness.

A 2012 Harvard study found students who practiced self-compassion after a disappointing exam were more motivated to try again than those who fixated on their failures. Instead of sinking into guilt, self-compassion allowed them to look with clear eyes at what went wrong, and to persist without being frozen by self-blame.

Another misunderstanding is that self-compassion is selfish. Yet, researchers repeatedly find that people who treat themselves kindly are also more kind and understanding with others. When your own tank is full, it's easier to genuinely support friends, family, and even strangers. Clinical psychologist Dr. Christopher Germer reminds us, "Self-compassion is simply giving the same kindness to ourselves that we would give to others."

In practice, self-compassion is courage in action. It means pausing when we're hurting and swapping out self-judgment for understanding. It isn't always easy, especially in a culture that glorifies toughness. But self-compassion isn't weakness—it's resilience rooted in empathy.

Recognizing and Challenging the Inner Critic

Before you can shift toward self-compassion, it helps to shine a light on your inner critic—the voice that points out your shortcomings, doubts your worth, and pushes harsh self-judgment. This internal voice can come from different places. Maybe you grew up with high expectations, or perhaps criticism from others has seeped into your own thoughts. Over time, you might find yourself repeating old, unkind scripts without even realizing it.

Start noticing the tone you use when you make a mistake or fall short. Do you call yourself names? Use words like "stupid," "lazy," or "failure"? Sometimes, the inner critic shouts, but other times it's sneakier, whispering that everyone else is better, or expecting you to be perfect.

Imagine, for a moment, a friend coming to you upset after a tough day. Would you speak to them the way you speak to yourself? Most people find that their tone is much gentler with others. This gap reveals how unfairly we sometimes treat ourselves.

Challenging the inner critic doesn't mean pretending you're perfect or ignoring problems. It means responding to yourself with balance. Instead of beating yourself up over a missed deadline, you might tell yourself, "That was hard, and I wish I had done better. But one mistake doesn't define who I am or what I can achieve next time."

Janelle's story offers a helpful example. She spent years berating herself at the slightest mistake, believing criticism would keep her sharp. Yet all it did was sap her confidence and energy. When she started paying attention, she realized her inner monologue sounded much harsher than any teacher or friend. With practice, Janelle began to pause and ask, "What would I say to someone I love right now?" Over time, the harsh voice softened, and she found herself bouncing back from setbacks more quickly.

Cognitive behavioral therapists encourage a simple exercise: write down some of your most common self-critical thoughts, and see if you'd say those things to a friend. If not, try rewriting the thought with the warmth you'd offer someone else. At first, this feels awkward or even forced, especially if you're used to harsh self-talk. But like any habit, challenging the inner critic grows easier with practice.

Practical Exercises for Building Self-Kindness

Building self-kindness isn't about ignoring mistakes or pretending everything is perfect. It's the practice of treating ourselves with the gentleness and support we need in difficult moments. There are several simple but powerful ways to nurture this skill, each aimed at rewiring responses toward more care and understanding.

A classic exercise is the "self-compassion break," created by Kristin Neff. When you notice you're being hard on yourself, try these three steps:

First, *notice* that you're struggling and name it: "This is a moment of pain," or "I'm feeling disappointed." Calling out our emotions brings them into the open, rather than stuffing them away. Just labeling what's going on helps soften the sting.

Second, *remind yourself that you're not alone*. Every human being messes up, gets rejected, or feels insecure sometimes. Try saying to yourself, "Struggle is part of being human," or "Others have felt this way too." This reminds us that suffering doesn't mean we're uniquely flawed—it means we're human.

Third, *offer yourself some kindness*. Place a hand over your heart, or give yourself a gentle squeeze on your arm. Whisper something soothing, like, "May I be gentle with myself," or, "It's okay to feel this way." Research shows that physical touch triggers the body's soothing system, lowering stress hormones and increasing feelings of safety.

For some, journaling can be a powerful tool. When self-criticism arises, write a letter to yourself as if you're your own best friend. Be honest about your struggles, but focus on support and understanding. Over time, these letters build a habit of self-kindness, even when your mood is low.

Visualization is another strategy. Picture someone who cares deeply for you—maybe a grandparent, teacher, or mentor. How would they respond to your pain? Imagine them speaking to you, offering comfort. Sometimes, borrowing another's voice helps soften your own.

There's evidence all around us that these approaches work. A study from the University of California found that college students who practiced self-compassion exercises for three weeks showed lower anxiety and depression, and greater well-being. The effect lasted, suggesting that small daily actions really do accumulate.

At first, these exercises can feel unnatural. Our brains are wired to notice threats, and self-criticism tries to protect us from failure, even if it makes us miserable. With intention and repetition, kindness starts to leave its footprint on the mind. Gradually, the automatic response in tough moments becomes softer, more understanding.

The Role of Mindfulness in Self-Compassion

It's hard to offer yourself compassion if you're not aware of what you're feeling. Sometimes, pain bubbles under the surface while you distract yourself with busyness or criticism. Mindfulness—the gentle art of noticing the present moment without judgment—creates the space where healing can begin.

When you practice mindfulness, you tune in to how you're feeling, just as you are. You don't try to push the discomfort away or get tangled in stories about not being good enough. You simply notice: "I feel anxious right now." Or, "There's sadness in my chest." This kind of awareness isn't passive; it opens a door to respond with care, rather than with reactivity.

Jon Kabat-Zinn, a pioneer in mindfulness research, describes it as "paying attention, on purpose, in the present moment, and non-judgmentally." This approach is at the heart of self-compassion. Only by acknowledging what hurts can we offer kindness to ourselves.

Many mindfulness practices are simple and accessible. By closing your eyes and focusing on your breath, you can notice each inhale and exhale, letting thoughts come and go without getting caught up in them. If critical thoughts emerge, you can greet them with curiosity, instead of anger or shame.

A helpful practice called "RAIN"—Recognize, Allow, Investigate, Nurture—can guide you through difficult emotions. Tara Brach, who popularized RAIN, suggests first *Recognizing* what you're feeling, *Allowing* it to be present, *Investigating* with gentle curiosity, and finally *Nurturing* yourself through words, touch, or breath. This flow wraps mindfulness and self-kindness together, offering a path through struggles rather than around them.

Research shows that even brief, daily mindfulness practices lower stress and increase resilience. In one experiment, participants who did a 10-minute mindfulness exercise each day described themselves as calmer and more self-accepting after just two weeks.

What's striking is that mindfulness isn't about "fixing" feelings, but making room for them. Sometimes emotions gently shift when observed with compassion; other times they linger, but become easier to hold. Either way, the simple act of noticing transforms your inner dialogue.

Integrating Self-Compassion into Everyday Life

It's one thing to practice self-compassion in quiet moments or guided exercises. Making it part of daily life is a richer challenge, especially when days are busy or stressful. Yet, the more we weave kindness into ordinary routines, the more it becomes second nature.

Start with the little moments. When you spill coffee or miss a bus, notice your first reaction. Do you react with frustration at yourself? See if you can pause and instead offer a brief, gentle word: "That's annoying, but it doesn't mean I'm a failure." Over time, these micro-moments rewire your brain's response to stress and mistakes.

In relationships, self-compassion helps us set boundaries and communicate with respect. When you're exhausted but feel pressure to say yes to every request, self-compassion encourages you to ask: "What do I need right now to take care of myself?" Granting yourself permission to rest or say no isn't selfish—it's responsible self-care.

In work or at school, perfectionism often tempts us to never be satisfied. Dr. Brené Brown, a leading researcher on vulnerability, shares: "Perfectionism is not the same thing as striving to be your best. Perfectionism is the belief that if we live perfect, look perfect, and act perfect, we can minimize or avoid the pain of blame, judgment, and shame." Self-compassion cuts through this trap by accepting that mistakes are part of growing, not a threat to our worth.

Celebrating small wins matters, too. When you notice yourself taking a kinder approach or bouncing back from self-criticism, pause and let that feeling register. Neuroscience tells us that when we savor moments of compassion, we reinforce those mental pathways, making it more natural to turn toward kindness next time.

It's also helpful to find supportive voices—whether in friends, mentors, or inspiring authors—who model self-compassion. Group mindfulness activities, peer support groups, or simple conversations about struggles can make kindness contagious. Stories of others' journeys remind us we're not alone, and they spark our own courage to be gentle with ourselves.

As you practice, there will still be days when the old inner critic returns louder than ever. That's not failure—it's simply being human. Self-compassion is a lifelong process, full of ups and downs. Each act of kindness, no matter how small, shapes the way we see ourselves and the world.

With time, the harsh voice quiets. In moments when pain or doubt arises, a gentler voice responds first. Instead of tightening with shame, your chest loosens. Instead of avoiding tough moments, you meet them with a steady hand. This transformation doesn't erase challenges, but it does soften the road ahead.

Healing and growth are never linear or simple. But through the steady practice of self-compassion—myth-busting, challenging your critic, building self-kindness, bringing in mindfulness, and folding it into daily life—you offer yourself a safe harbor. In that harbor, courage and joy are free to flourish. And while storms may still come, you'll know your own support stands ready, patient and kind.

Chapter 9

When the world feels loud, confusing, or even unkind, there is something profoundly comforting about retreating to a quiet spot, opening a notebook or laptop, and letting words flow. Journaling can become so much more than a record of days gone by or a list of things to do. It becomes a shelter—soft, timeless, and uniquely yours. In this place, thoughts and feelings that seem too complicated or tangled to say aloud can find their shape in ink and paper. Here, processing takes the place of judgment. Here, truth feels safe enough to stretch out and breathe.

Understanding the Journal as a Safe Haven

A journal isn't just a stack of blank pages. Think of it as a room no one else can enter without your permission—a space you decorate with your memories, dreams, disappointments, and hopes. It offers a kind of protection; what you write is just for you unless or until you choose to share it. Within its covers, you can be honest in a way that feels risky elsewhere.

Researchers at the University of Texas have

highlighted how private writing can help people cope with difficult events. Dr. James Pennebaker, a leader in expressive writing research, found that people facing trauma often experienced better emotional health after writing about their experiences privately. This effect isn't only for the most serious moments—students writing about stressful school events, adults processing the end of a friendship, or someone dealing with a minor mistake all benefit. Perhaps it's because the journal acts as a buffer. It listens, but never interrupts. It holds pain without passing judgment.

Many people describe a sense of relief at the end of a long journal entry, like letting out a breath they didn't know they were holding. The act of writing, in and of itself, provides a moment to step away from the outside world. While friends and family can be wonderful sources of comfort and advice, a journal's greatest gift is how it lets you hear yourself—honestly, without distractions.

Processing Raw Emotions and Difficult Memories

Not every feeling fits inside a neat box. Grief, anger, jealousy, confusion—some emotions spill over, unpredictable and messy. Yet in the privacy of a journal, you can let these feelings out exactly as they are. You don't have to worry about saying the right thing. You don't have to package your emotion in a way someone else will understand. You just write.

Take, for example, the experience of Olivia. She lost her grandmother—her best friend and confidant. Talking about it felt impossible. When people asked how she was, she'd mumble "okay" and change the subject. But her journal became a place where no answer was too messy. She wrote letters to her grandmother. She wrote about the loneliness, the memories, and the anger at how unfair it all seemed. She wrote, "I hate that I can't hear your laugh anymore," one September evening. No one else saw those words, but through writing them, something inside her softened. Gradually, the words shifted from anger to remembering happy moments, until, one day, she recognized that she felt a little lighter.

Researchers have shown that "affect labeling"—the process of putting emotional experiences into words—can calm the brain and aid emotional regulation. In other words, when you name and write about a feeling, it often becomes a little less overwhelming. The anxiety that chewed away at the corners of your mind, the sadness that colored every day gray, takes on a new form—something you can see and understand, not just something you feel.

Difficult memories, too, can lose some of their sharp edges through journaling. Maya Angelou famously said, "There is no greater agony than bearing an untold story inside you." In writing, even memories that bring pain can be softened. Journaling does not erase what happened, and it's not about forcing optimism or pretending all is well. It is about giving your memories a place to live outside your head so that they don't hold you hostage.

Some people use prompts to get started: "What's a moment I can't forget, and how do I feel about it now?" Others simply allow themselves to write freely, letting one sentence lead to the next without a plan. Whichever you choose, the act of writing transforms raw emotions. The page accepts what the world sometimes cannot.

Shifting Perspective—Reframing Experiences Through Writing

Journaling is not just for venting. It can help change how you see your experiences. When pain, frustration, or embarrassment gets put on paper, it makes room for curiosity. "Can I look at this moment as a lesson, rather than a failure? Is there a strength in me I didn't see before?" Through writing, you start to ask new questions.

Cognitive behavioral therapy, one of the most trusted methods for treating anxiety and depression, often employs a similar technique called "cognitive reappraisal." Dr. Aaron Beck, who developed this therapy, encouraged people to notice their automatic thoughts and gently challenge them. With a journal, you can do the same, becoming your own gentle guide. You might write about a time you felt left out at a party, and after the anger and hurt, you may ask, "What else could have been happening?" Maybe others were just shy, too. Perhaps the feeling of isolation says more about your own fears than about how others see you.

You can try writing about the same event twice—from your perspective and from someone else's. This exercise, suggested by many writing therapists, can unlock compassion, even for those who have hurt you. The simple act of seeing the situation from a new angle can make it feel less personal or permanent.

Anyone who's ever reread an old diary knows the strange, bittersweet joy of realizing you once obsessed over something that now barely matters. This, in itself, is proof that emotions and struggles change with time and reflection. One entry might gush, "I'll never get over this," visible in slanted, tear-blotted script. The next year, you laugh at your younger self's intensity. Such moments aren't about mocking past pain but about noticing your growth. With every page, your view of the world—and your place in it—expands.

Identifying Patterns: From Pain Points to Personal Growth

Once your thoughts and feelings are written down, patterns start to emerge. You may notice you feel anxious every Sunday night. Or that arguments with loved ones follow the same script each time. Sometimes, these patterns are impossible to spot until you see them written over several pages or weeks.

Samantha, now a high school senior, began journaling in middle school. At first, it was a private venting method for when a friend upset her or when she felt invisible at home. After months of writing, she began to notice a repeated phrase in her entries: "I wish they would just notice me." She realized that her greatest pain wasn't the specific fight or slight—it was feeling unseen. Once identified, that pain became something she could work with directly. She started nurturing herself with positive affirmations, working on her self-esteem, and having more honest talks with her parents and friends.

Identifying patterns through journaling allows you to connect the dots between what happens in your life and your internal reactions. Peer-reviewed studies show that this kind of self-awareness leads to healthier decision-making. Dr. Susan David, a psychologist at Harvard Medical School, writes, "Emotional agility—handling your inner world with curiosity and compassion—starts with recognizing patterns in your thoughts and feelings." Your journal becomes a tool for developing this agility.

Pattern-seeking has its roots in our biology. The human brain is wired to search for meaning. When something hurts, we naturally want to understand why. Writing offers proof: "I feel exhausted whenever I say yes too quickly" or "I get inspired when I'm outside." Patterns, once discovered, become keys that can open doors to self-care, improved relationships, and creative growth.

Of course, seeing the pattern is only the first step. The real transformation comes when you decide to act on these discoveries.

Transforming Insights into Actionable Empowerment

If there is a superpower hidden in a journal, it is transformation. Once you have poured out your feelings, reframed your story, and spotted the patterns, the next question is: What now? This, perhaps, is where many people find the greatest empowerment. It's not just about knowing yourself; it's about using what you learn.

Journaling can help you set intentions, design goals, or map out personal changes. Let's say you noticed you often write about feeling too tired for your favorite hobbies. What might you do with that insight? Maybe it's time to start protecting time for the activities that bring you joy. Or, if you spot a rhythm of self-doubt whenever you face new challenges, you might try writing affirmations or listing examples of times you overcame adversity.

Experts like Brené Brown, researcher and author, emphasize the connection between vulnerability and courage. "Vulnerability is the birthplace of innovation, creativity, and change," she says. By being vulnerable with yourself in a journal, you make space for your next brave steps.

Some people use their journal to create action lists: "Three ways I can nurture myself this week," or "One small risk I will take today." Others write letters to their future selves or script out conversations they need to have. The power is always in the doing, but the page makes the doing feel not just possible, but personal.

Real transformation isn't always dramatic. Sometimes it's choosing to treat yourself with a little more kindness. Sometimes it means getting help or asking for support. At its heart, journaling is a practice in listening—to your hurts and hopes, your dreams and doubts. In listening, you find clarity. In clarity, you find the courage to change.

Each page you fill is a testament to the fact that your story matters. The act of writing becomes a quiet revolution, turning pain into wisdom and fear into action. There, within your journal, you craft not just your story, but your future—one word at a time. The sanctuary you build with your own hands becomes a springboard for growth, strength, and unstoppable possibility.

Chapter 10

There is a quiet, gentle kind of courage that forms when you learn to set boundaries. It's not a loud or showy defiance; instead, it feels more like a deep breath that fills your lungs after being cramped for too long. When you claim your space with grace and strength, you allow room for your truest self to grow—unhindered, unashamed, and free.

Understanding the Importance of Boundaries—Why They Matter for Well-Being

Most people don't realize just how much their happiness hinges on the invisible lines they draw. Boundaries are the lines we set—sometimes whispered, sometimes fiercely declared—that communicate what we will and will not accept. Without them, our lives can become a jumble of yeses we never wanted to give.

Brené Brown, a professor and bestselling author, once said, "Daring to set boundaries is about having the courage to love ourselves, even when we risk disappointing others." Imagine your life as a garden. If you never mark off the space, anyone can trample through, picking and plucking as they please, often leaving your flowers wilted and the soil compacted. With boundaries, you plant a gentle fence, not to keep people out entirely, but to protect what matters inside.

Studies have shown that people who maintain healthy boundaries experience better mental health, less stress, and more fulfilling relationships. In a 2022 study published in the Journal of Positive Psychology, researchers found that college students who practiced assertive boundary-setting reported greater confidence and lower rates of anxiety. This isn't a coincidence. Our emotional well-being depends on knowing—and acting on—what feels right for us.

Boundaries do more than protect us from harm. They help us grow. They nurture respect, not just from others but from ourselves. Without boundaries, resentment can sneak in, whispering that you're taken for granted or ignored. Over time, this can eat away at your happiness, turning relationships sour. On the other hand, clear, consistent boundaries help you feel safe, respected, and valued.

Boundaries aren't selfish. They're an act of self-respect. Consider the bestselling memoirist Glennon Doyle, who writes, "Every time you're given a choice between disappointing someone else and disappointing yourself, your duty is to disappoint that someone else." Each time you choose what's right for you, you teach others how you deserve to be treated and remind yourself that your needs matter.

This doesn't always come easily. Many of us have been taught, directly or indirectly, that putting others first is the mark of goodness. But when you constantly ignore your own needs, you lose sight of yourself. The people you love end up with a faded version of you, too tired or resentful to truly connect.

The truth is, setting boundaries isn't about shutting out the world. It's about opening up space where you—and your relationships—can thrive.

Identifying Your Limits—Recognizing Where You Need Space

But how are you supposed to know what your boundaries even are? Sometimes, we've spent so much time trying to keep others happy that our own wants and limits have faded. The first step is tuning in, listening for the quiet signals your mind and body send you every day.

Think about the last time you agreed to something and then immediately felt tense or uneasy. Maybe you promised to help a classmate with a project, even though you already had plans. Or perhaps you let a friend borrow your favorite book—for the third time—even though you hadn't finished reading it. That discomfort is your body's way of nudging you, hinting that a line has been crossed.

Another clue comes when anger simmers just below the surface. You might notice yourself feeling irritated after spending time with someone who never seems to listen. Or maybe sadness creeps in when you're constantly overlooked at family gatherings. These moments are your inner compass, quietly pointing at situations where your space is being squeezed.

Take a few minutes to reflect on times when you felt drained or frustrated after interacting with someone. Ask yourself: What part of this interaction felt wrong? When did I wish I had spoken up? Was I hoping someone would notice how uncomfortable I was?

Marianne, a high school sophomore, recalls always being the one her friends turned to with their problems. She cared deeply about her group but after a while, she felt exhausted and anxious after every conversation. "I realized I never had a chance to talk about what was going on with me," she says. "It was like I was just a sponge for their worries." For Marianne, the feeling of depletion was a sign that she needed to set limits around how—and when—she supported others.

Boundaries look different for everyone. For some, it's saying no to extra work when evenings are meant for family. For others, it's turning off notifications after 8 p.m. so your mind can rest. For parents, it could be carving out twenty minutes of alone time in the morning. Each person has a unique threshold, and the process of discovering yours takes trial and error.

Writing down moments when you wish you'd responded differently helps. Dr. Nedra Glover Tawwab, a licensed therapist, suggests journaling about situations that left you feeling uncomfortable, resentful, or overwhelmed. She writes, "Notice what your mind and body are trying to communicate and honor those signals."

Pay attention to patterns. If you regularly feel anxious before meetings, perhaps you need more structure or fewer spontaneous requests. If certain friendships leave you feeling like you're "too much" or "not enough," those relationships might need clearer boundaries.

It's also helpful to check your physical responses. Tight shoulders, headaches, or a heavy feeling in your chest are all signs that something is not right. Our bodies often notice violations before our minds do. Trust those instincts—even when they're hard to interpret.

Learning where you need space isn't selfish. It's the first step to showing up authentically and fully for yourself, and, in the end, for others.

Communicating Boundaries Assertively and Respectfully

Knowing what your boundaries are is only the beginning. The next challenge is expressing them. For many, this is the hardest part. Saying no or speaking up, especially to people you care about or those in authority, can feel like standing on a stage with all eyes on you.

But expressing your boundaries doesn't have to be dramatic. In fact, the most effective boundaries are stated calmly, simply, and without apology. Dr. Henry Cloud, co-author of the book *Boundaries*, puts it plainly: "You get what you tolerate." If you say nothing, others will continue to treat you in the same way. If you speak up, clearly and without anger, you begin to shape new expectations.

It's helpful to remember that assertiveness is not the same as aggressiveness. Assertiveness means standing up for yourself while also respecting the needs and feelings of others. For instance, instead of snapping, "Stop bothering me!" you might say, "I need some quiet time right now, but I'd be happy to talk to you later." This approach acknowledges both your needs and the other person's desire to connect.

A key part of healthy communication is using "I" statements. For example, "I feel overwhelmed when plans change at the last minute. Can we schedule things earlier in the week?" The focus is on your feelings and your requests, rather than blaming or shaming the other person. This keeps the conversation open and reduces defensiveness.

Sometimes, people worry that stating boundaries will

make them seem rude or difficult. But consider the alternative. Unspoken expectations often lead to simmering resentment or sudden blow-ups. Both options hurt relationships more than a few moments of mild discomfort.

Raj, a college freshman, struggled with this at first. He wanted to fit in and didn't want to let his roommate down. But he often found himself agreeing to late-night study sessions even when he desperately needed sleep. Finally, after a sleepless week, he said, "Hey, I'm going to have to turn in early tonight. I need rest to be at my best during the day." To his relief, his roommate was understanding, and things felt easier after that.

Being honest about what you need isn't just good for you—it also teaches others how to interact with you. You become more predictable, easier to trust, and more pleasant to be around. People don't have to guess what you'll tolerate or wonder if you're secretly upset.

Remember, you're not responsible for managing other people's feelings—only your own. If someone feels briefly disappointed, it doesn't mean you did something wrong. Family therapist Terri Cole reminds us, "Healthy boundaries are not walls. They are the gates and fences that allow you to enjoy the beauty of your own garden." Speak from a place of care, both for yourself and the relationship, and know that discomfort is often just the growing pains of healthier ways of connecting.

Sometimes, if you feel uncertain or anxious, it helps to rehearse what you want to say. This can be in front of a mirror, with a friend, or by writing it down. Over time, speaking up becomes easier. Each small success builds your confidence.

Boundary-setting is not a one-time announcement, but an ongoing conversation—a way of interacting with the world that grows stronger every time you choose to honor yourself.

Navigating Pushback—Responding to Boundary Violations with Confidence

Setting boundaries can feel like a quiet revolution in your life, but not everyone will celebrate the change right away. Sometimes, when you start protecting your time and energy, others push back. They might question your seriousness, try to guilt you, or simply ignore what you've said.

This reaction is natural. If someone isn't used to hearing "no" from you, your new firmness might surprise or disappoint them. However, that doesn't mean your boundaries are wrong or that you need to explain yourself endlessly.

Psychologist Dr. Lisa Firestone points out, "When others resist your boundaries, it's often because they benefited from you not having any." She explains that pushback is a sign you're moving in the right direction. After all, the goal is not to prevent all discomfort but to create respectful, sustainable dynamics.

Consider the experience of Jordan, who always loaned out his homework to friends even though it made him uneasy. The first time he declined, saying, "I can't share my assignments anymore; I want to do my own work," his friends got annoyed. They teased him, called him selfish, and threatened to leave him out of group plans. Jordan felt hurt, but he also noticed a new sense of pride. He realized he was protecting his time and his integrity.

Dealing with pushback often involves staying calm, repeating your boundary, and not rushing to justify or overexplain. This is sometimes called the "broken record" technique. For example:

— "I can't lend money right now."
— "I know you're upset, but my answer hasn't changed."
— "I need this weekend for myself."

The conversation might be uncomfortable, but your steady response does more than just defend your line. It shows that you take yourself seriously—and that you expect others to, as well.

Sometimes a person will try to negotiate, offering small exceptions or trying to make you feel guilty.

Guilt is a powerful feeling—one that can cloud your judgment and make you doubt your own needs. When this happens, pause and check in with yourself. Are you tempted to say yes just to keep the peace or make someone else happy? Or are you honoring what's genuinely best for you?

It can also help to affirm your boundary to yourself. Remind yourself why this line matters. Recall how much better you felt after honoring your limits in the past. Trust that real friends, family, and colleagues will ultimately respect your decision, even if it takes time.

Of course, there are situations that call for flexibility. If a close friend or family member is struggling, you might choose to bend without breaking. The key is to make the choice, not to feel forced or coerced.

During especially tough moments, you might want to lean on allies—friends, mentors, or counselors who support your choices. Sharing your experiences with someone you trust can make a world of difference, helping you process feelings and stand firm when others push back.

Boundaries that are enforced consistently over time become easier for others to accept. Each time you say yes to yourself, you make it easier to withstand the pressure, guilt, or manipulation that sometimes comes your way.

Sustaining Healthy Boundaries—Maintaining

Consistency Over Time

Setting a boundary is only half the work; the other half is honoring it, even when the novelty wears off or life gets busy again. In fact, the healthiest boundaries are lived out in the small, everyday decisions far more than in grand, dramatic stands.

There's something quietly powerful about doing what you said you would do—being the kind of person whose actions match their words. Consistency not only makes life more predictable for you, it also helps others trust and respect your boundaries.

But maintaining your limits can be tricky, especially as relationships shift and new situations appear. You might find it easy to say no at first, only to slip back into old habits when you're tired or when others seem disappointed. This is normal. Restoring and strengthening boundaries is an ongoing process, not a one-time event.

One way to keep boundaries strong is to check in with yourself regularly. Are you feeling more energized and content, or have resentment and exhaustion crept back in? Sometimes, a boundary needs to be adjusted as your life changes. What worked in one season might not feel right in another.

Lara, a junior in college, once thought she had her boundaries figured out. She attended every family event, even when it meant missing out on time with friends. It wasn't until she missed a close friend's birthday that she realized her boundaries needed tweaking. "I learned that I had to balance family time with what mattered to me. No one else could decide that but me." For Lara, adjusting her limits helped her find more balance and peace.

Self-care plays a critical role in keeping your boundaries clear and healthy. Taking time to rest, eat well, and pursue your own interests sends a strong message that you value yourself. When your "tank" is full, it's easier to make decisions that honor your needs.

It's also important to give yourself grace when you slip. Everyone falters sometimes. Maybe you agreed to a last-minute obligation or forgot to take a break when you needed one. Instead of beating yourself up, treat these moments as chances to learn. Think about what was hard in the moment and how you might respond differently next time.

Celebrating small victories helps, too. Each time you advocate for yourself, whether it's in a big way or with a quiet no, you reinforce your self-trust. Over time, these moments add up, laying the groundwork for stronger, more resilient relationships.

A sense of freedom grows from that consistency. You'll notice it in small ways—the relief of not having to make excuses, the ease of moving through your day without guilt, and the expanding sense of possibility when you choose what aligns with your values.

Others around you also begin to shift. Clear boundaries teach people how to treat you. Over time, most will adjust to the new normal, letting go of expectations that don't fit. The relationships that remain are those built on real respect and understanding.

Boundaries are not rigid lines drawn in the sand but are living, flexible guides that grow with you. Some may shift or soften, while others become firmer. What matters most is that they are true to who you are, and that they allow you to move through life with both kindness and power.

Claiming your space is not an act of separation but one of connection—to yourself and to those you care about most. It's in these spaces, honoring both your needs and the needs of others, that you find the richest ground for your life and relationships to flourish. The grace with which you hold your boundaries becomes a quiet invitation for everyone around you to honor themselves more boldly, too.

Chapter 11

Most of us know what it feels like when emotions seem to take over, hijacking our words and actions in the blink of an eye. Maybe your heart pounds, words tumble out, and only after the heat dies down do you wonder why you said or did that. That rush—that surge of feeling and instant reaction—is familiar to everyone. Yet there's another path, one that puts a gentle hand on the shoulder of our impulses, whispering, "Wait. Maybe there's another way." This chapter is about finding and taking that path.

It's not just about stopping yourself from doing something you regret later. It's about learning, with real techniques and daily practice, how to move from reacting out of habit to responding with choice and clarity. This isn't some mystical secret. It's a skill, and like any skill, it can be learned—and even fun to practice.

Understanding the Difference: Reaction vs. Response

Imagine you're in class, and someone makes a comment that stings. It lands hard, and you feel your muscles tense, a retort forming before you even think. That's reaction. It's automatic, almost like a reflex when the doctor taps your knee with that funny little hammer. It's driven by habit, old wiring, survival instincts, and—sometimes—stories about ourselves we didn't even realize we believed.

But response—that's different. It's like seeing a fork in the road and choosing which way you want to go. When you respond, you have a moment to see what's happening inside you. You get curious, notice the rush of heat or the ache in your stomach. You don't deny it, but you don't let it control you, either. Instead, you pause. You take a slow breath. You might choose to ask a question, to wait before you speak, or simply to let the moment pass.

Dr. Viktor Frankl, a psychiatrist and Holocaust survivor, once wrote, "Between stimulus and response, there is a space. In that space is our power to choose our response. In our response lies our growth and our freedom." That space is where mindfulness lives. The more you build it, the easier it becomes to spot your reactions before they decide your next move.

It's worth noting that everyone reacts at times. The goal isn't to become some emotionless robot but to give yourself room to choose rather than always falling into the same old patterns. The difference between reacting and responding may seem small, but on the ground, it can feel like the difference between chaos and calm.

The Science of Mindfulness and Its Impact on Emotional Regulation

It might be tempting to dismiss mindfulness as just a trend—some passing fad with little real impact. But look at the science, and the story deepens considerably. Mindfulness, at its heart, means paying attention to the moment you're in, on purpose and without judgment. When researchers peek inside the brain with all their clever tools, they see something fascinating: practicing mindfulness actually changes the way our brains process emotion.

Take the amygdala, for example. It's often called the brain's "alarm system," the part that sounds the siren when we feel threatened or anxious. In people who make time for mindfulness practices—even just a few minutes each day—the amygdala becomes less reactive, according to studies from Harvard and others. This means that big emotions may still come, but they don't run the show quite so easily.

Meanwhile, other parts of the brain—like the prefrontal cortex, the area right behind your forehead—start to take a more active role. The prefrontal cortex is like a wise coach, helping you plan, problem-solve, and weigh consequences. When it's more engaged, you're more likely to notice when you're spiraling and to step back instead of getting swept away.

A study published in the journal *Emotion* found that just eight weeks of mindfulness meditation helped participants respond to stress with less emotional reactivity. They could recover more quickly after upsetting events and were less likely to ruminate on what had happened. In fact, schools that have introduced mindfulness programs often report improvements in student focus, behavior, and emotional wellbeing.

It's not just about stress or anger, either. Mindfulness seems to help with everything from test anxiety to relationships with family and friends. Professor Jon Kabat-Zinn, who created one of the first mindfulness-based stress reduction programs, puts it simply: "You can't stop the waves, but you can learn to surf." Science gives us reason to believe that's more than just a nice idea—it's a practice that can literally reshape your brain.

Core Mindfulness Techniques for Creating Space Between Stimulus and Action

So, how do you start to build that space Dr. Frankl talked about—the space that separates a gut reaction from a thoughtful response? The answer isn't complicated. In fact, it starts with something so simple that it's often overlooked: the breath.

One core technique is mindful breathing. The way it works is nothing fancy. Whenever you notice a big emotion rising or you sense yourself about to snap, direct your attention to the feeling of air moving in and out of your body. Notice your chest expanding, your belly rising and falling, the coolness of your inhale and the warmth of your exhale. This isn't about changing your breath, just observing it. As your attention anchors to your breath, even if only for a few seconds, you create the smallest of pauses.

Some people find grounding exercises incredibly helpful. This might mean pushing your feet against the floor, noticing the sensation of the ground supporting you, or scanning your body rapidly from head to toe, becoming aware of physical feeling rather than the swirl of thoughts. Sometimes just naming what's happening—"I'm feeling really angry"—can switch on a more analytical part of the brain, cooling the intensity enough to choose what comes next.

Another practice, called the "STOP" technique, takes you through four easy steps: Stop, Take a breath, Observe, Proceed. When something triggers you, pause for a beat. Take one slow, deliberate breath. Observe what's happening inside—tight shoulders, racing heart, biting words on the tip of your tongue. Then, only after that, proceed with whatever action feels right. This little sequence can be repeated so often that, eventually, it almost does itself.

For those who need something more visual, imagine a traffic light. Red for "stop," yellow for "wait and notice," and green for "respond with intention." Even picturing a stop sign in your mind can help break the cycle of immediate reacting.

Dr. Daniel Siegel, an expert in interpersonal neurobiology, explains the idea simply: "When you name it, you can tame it." Bringing awareness to your inner experience is the first step. You don't have to judge or fix it, just notice.

These practices aren't magic. They won't erase anger or sadness or embarrassment. Instead, they help you meet those feelings as they arrive, rather than after they've kicked down the door and started rearranging your life.

Practical Exercises: Training the Mind to Pause and Reframe

Building the habit of responding instead of reacting takes time, but it is absolutely possible. Many people start with just a few minutes each day, gradually adding mindfulness into ordinary life moments rather than saving it for a special hour set aside in silence. Here are some detailed exercises that make the difference real.

Breath Counting Exercise:
Sit quietly, close your eyes, and begin counting your breaths. Inhale—one. Exhale—two. Continue counting upwards, paying close attention to each breath. If your mind drifts, gently return to the count. Try to reach ten breaths without losing focus. If you do,

simply start over. This builds the mental muscle of returning to the present, a skill you'll use whenever strong emotions threaten to sweep you away.

Mindful "Mini-Pause":
Throughout the day, set a reminder—perhaps using a phone alarm or a sticky note—to pause for ten seconds. When the chime goes off, stop whatever you're doing. Notice one thing you can see, one thing you can hear, and one sensation in your body. This tiny break helps create a natural disconnect from automatic behaviors, making it easier to notice and shift how you're about to respond.

Reframing Through Self-Talk:
When you catch yourself thinking, "I always mess up" or "That person did this on purpose," pause and try to reframe. Ask yourself, "Is that 100% true?" What might another explanation be? What would I say to a friend in this moment? This gentle questioning can transform the trap of reaction into the freedom of choosing a different path.

The "Urge Surfing" Technique:
When a big urge or emotion builds, imagine it like a wave. Instead of fighting or obeying it immediately, just notice what it feels like in your body—the tension, the energy, the movement. Watch it, breathe with it, and picture yourself riding the wave as it rises, crests, and falls. Urges, like waves, don't last forever. This practice helps you see that emotions, no matter how strong, will pass.

Gratitude Journaling:
At the end of each day, jot down three moments when you felt pulled to react, whether you did or not. Briefly write what happened and how you handled it. Over time, you'll see your brain naturally start to spot patterns, giving you more data to work with and celebrate the times you chose response instead of reaction.

These exercises may seem simple—and they are—but repetition cements new pathways in the brain. Each time you choose to pause, even for a split second, you flex the mental muscles needed to transform impulsive reactions into wise, skillful responses.

Real-Life Applications: Turning Triggers into Opportunities for Thoughtful Response

Knowing these tools is one thing; using them in messy, everyday situations is where the work—and the magic—happens. Consider Eli, a high school sophomore whose temper flares whenever his younger sister borrows his things without asking. He used to storm into her room, ready to blast accusations, until he started trying mindful pauses. The first time he used a deep breath and named the tightness in his chest, he didn't say anything. It felt awkward, maybe even a little weak. Yet ten minutes later, when the edge had softened, he found himself talking to his sister in a tone that surprised even him—not full of blame, but curious and honest about what bothered him.

Stories like Eli's are not rare. In classrooms, students who practice mindful techniques are shown to interrupt cycles of teasing or gossip, stopping to notice if their urge to laugh along really matches their values. Mindfulness gives you a chance to step back and ask: "Is this who I want to be right now?" Even parents and teachers, whose patience is tried a hundred times a day, find they can ride out frustration, choosing kind firmness over sharp words.

Dr. Susan David, psychologist and author of *Emotional Agility*, explains, "Between how we feel and what we do, there is a space. And in that space is the power to make choices based on our values." The idea isn't to shut down your feelings, but to honor them—while still making conscious choices about how you want to act.

Trigger moments aren't always dramatic, either. Sometimes they're the slow build—traffic backing up, deadlines stacking, texts going unanswered. In these quieter moments, pause practices are just as essential. They help prevent the build-up that can eventually lead to an explosion.

One study that followed people who practiced mindfulness-based stress reduction (MBSR) found that participants reported fewer instances of "acting contrary" to their true selves. They didn't stop feeling impulses or anger; instead, they got better at pausing before those emotions translated into actions they'd regret.

Take Jamie, a teacher who faced a difficult parent. Before learning any mindfulness, Jamie might have been dismissive or defensive during a tough phone call. Instead, she tried a grounding exercise, feeling her feet on the floor and reminding herself, "I am listening. I am safe." The conversation was still intense, but Jamie managed to steer it toward solutions instead of spiraling into blame.

Athletes use this skill too, learning to step back in high-pressure moments, read their body's signals, and channel nerves into sharper focus rather than panicked errors. Musicians, actors, even emergency responders—anyone who faces high-stakes moments—benefits from this space between feeling and doing.

When these practices become woven into daily life, they have ripple effects. Friendships become less dramatic. Arguments are shorter or avoided entirely. Apologies come more easily, and self-compassion grows. Even when things go wrong—and they always will—you're less likely to torture yourself afterward, because you've seen the power of response over reaction.

The truth is, you won't always catch yourself in time. Sometimes you'll react before you remember to breathe, and that's perfectly human. Yet, with practice, the pause between stimulus and response stretches further each time, and the mind gets used to choosing the path of response over reaction.

Every time you meet a trigger with curiosity rather than judgment or fear, you rewrite the story you tell about yourself. You're not someone forever at the mercy of whatever happens around you. You're someone who can pause, notice, and respond—a creator, not just a passenger, in the unfolding of your life.

This isn't a promise of perfection, but of new possibilities, born from thousands of tiny choices. The way you meet each moment can shift, sometimes just slightly, yet over time, those shifts add up to a whole different experience of yourself and your relationships. The ability to pause is a gift you give yourself—and, in turn, to everyone you meet.

Chapter 12

Sometimes, in the quiet of night, the glow from our screens feels oddly comforting. We scroll, tap, like, repeat—a rhythm that has become second nature. Each swipe brings us smiles to borrow, adventures to dream about, and sometimes, a fleeting pang of doubt. Why does their life seem brighter, happier, more complete? As connections multiply, comparisons bloom in the garden of our minds.

Understanding the Comparison Trap: How Social Media Shapes Our Self-Perception

It's easy to forget that social media began as a way to connect people, but for many, it's become a place where we hold up our lives and measure them against a seemingly perfect standard. The more we scroll, the more we see fragments of other people's highlight reels: the trip to Tokyo, the straight-A report card, the flawless skin, the friend group packed with inside jokes. It all looks so effortless.

Dr. Melissa Hunt, a psychologist at the University of Pennsylvania, points out, "Social media isn't inherently bad. But when we use it to judge ourselves, it can chip away at our self-esteem." This quiet erosion happens one post at a time. Studies support Dr. Hunt's perspective. A national poll from the American Psychological Association found that teens and young adults who spend over two hours a day on social media are more likely to experience feelings of inadequacy and sadness compared to those who use it less.

Why is that? Social media platforms are engineered to show us what's popular, what's beautiful, what's successful. Algorithms prioritize posts with sparkling beaches over cloudy days, triumphs over setbacks. Over time, brains conditioned to notice differences start to magnify our own flaws. Scrolling turns from amusement to what feels like a performance review, where the only metric is how we stack up against others.

Maya, a high school sophomore, once described opening her phone as "walking into a party where everyone is amazing except me." That's the comparison trap—when admiration of someone else's story shifts into a harsh critique of our own. This isn't to say social media is a villain. But understanding the comparison trap lets us loosen its grip.

Self-perception is fragile, especially in the digital age. When every scroll is a fresh opportunity to judge our journeys against others, the noise in our heads can drown out our own unique voice. Recognizing the comparison game is the first step to escaping it. Once we see the mechanics, we can start to reshape our online experience.

Spotting Signals: Identifying Content That Uplifts vs. Content That Drains

Not all content leaves us feeling the same. Some posts encourage us, make us laugh, or ignite curiosity. Others, though, can pull us into a spiral of heaviness and inadequacy, often without us even noticing. Learning to sense the difference matters.

Imagine your mind as a garden—some seeds blossom, others spread weeds before you realize what's happening. Start to notice how you feel after seeing different types of posts. Does watching someone's morning routine inspire you to create your own healthy habits, or does it make you feel behind? Does a classmate's art project spark ideas, or does it silence your creative confidence? These subtle feelings whisper important truths about what feeds—or depletes—your spirit.

A study by the Pew Research Center found that 71% of teens have felt excluded or left out after viewing posts about events they missed. The data matches what intuition tells us: certain types of content can leave invisible bruises. On the flip side, psychologist Dr. Susan David shares that "joy is contagious—when we surround ourselves with positive and supportive messages, our mood and self-belief often improve."

Learning to spot the difference can be as simple as pausing after a scroll. Are you smiling and energized, or tense and anxious? Is your mind buzzing with possibilities or tangled with self-doubt? Some people even keep a small journal near their phone, jotting down how certain content makes them feel.

Try this: For one week, be mindful when online. At the end of each session, write down three words that describe your mood. Notice the patterns. Unfollow or mute pages that consistently leave you feeling less-than. Celebrate those that boost your spirits or teach you something new. You don't have to be ruthless, just intentional.

What helps most is realizing that inspiration grows stronger when we feel seen and encouraged, not when we feel small. Knowing which signals uplift you means you can choose your digital company as carefully as you'd choose your friends in real life.

Curating Your Feed for Inspiration: Practical Steps to Build a Positive Online Space

Once you've learned to recognize what lifts you up and what weighs you down, it's time to become the gardener of your own digital world. Curating your feed isn't just about following or unfollowing people at random—it's about deliberately shaping your online environment to serve your growth, not your anxieties.

Start with a purge—a gentle one. Scroll through your followers and ask yourself: does this person or page add value to my life? Do their posts make me smile, think, or motivate me? If the answer is consistently no, consider muting or unfollowing. Remember, it's not personal; it's about protecting your well-being.

Research published in Computers in Human Behavior suggests that people who actively curate their feeds—for example, by following accounts focused on creativity, positivity, or helpful advice—report higher levels of happiness and self-confidence. Even small adjustments can have big effects. Swap out celebrity highlight reels for artists, activists, or writers who share honest struggles as well as triumphs. Look for voices that reflect a range of stories, backgrounds, and experiences.

Odessa, a 17-year-old aspiring writer, described what happened when she did a "feed refresh." "I replaced all the influencers who made me feel bad about my body with accounts that talk openly about mental health, writing motivation, and social justice," she shared. "My phone felt lighter, and so did I."

You can also add pockets of inspiration to your everyday feed. Try following pages that post uplifting quotes, mindfulness exercises, or even cute animal videos—whatever reliably charges your happiness battery. Make an effort to seek out creators who don't just share glossy outcomes, but messy middles and lessons learned. Some people even curate "close friends" lists or private highlight reels to control what content they see most often.

Another tactic is setting boundaries around your social media use. Schedule breaks, turn off push notifications, and avoid checking your feed first or last thing in the day. Dr. Jean Twenge, a psychology professor at San Diego State University, recommends carving out "screen-free" zones or hours, especially before bedtime: "A break from constant digital input allows you to recharge, reflect, and return online with a clear mind."

You are allowed to be choosy. Imagine your feed like your bedroom or workspace—you wouldn't fill it with things that make you uneasy or insecure. Fill your online world with what feels like sunlight: people who celebrate others, pages that push you to grow, and content that refreshes your mind.

Building Genuine Connections: Engaging with Communities Rather Than Competitors

So often, social media feels like an endless contest. Who has the most followers? The most likes? The prettiest pictures? But the beating heart of these platforms—beneath the numbers and filters—is the chance to connect, not compete.

Community is built when people gather around a shared purpose or interest, supporting each other through ups and downs. Author Brené Brown writes,

"Connection is why we're here. We are hardwired to connect with others, it's what gives purpose and meaning to our lives." Social media gives us a chance to find our people—whether they share an interest in K-pop, science, social change, or wild rollercoaster rides.

Louisa, age sixteen, found a group for young climate activists online. "Instead of just seeing people as competition for scholarships or awards, we're trading ideas and supporting each other's projects. We talk about setbacks, not just wins," she explains. This sense of community turned what could have been comparison into collaboration.

Don't be afraid to reach out and engage. Comment thoughtfully, share encouragement, ask genuine questions. Many creators and participants cherish meaningful engagement over mindless likes. When you contribute real value, you're remembered—and inspired. Experts recommend starting small: respond to an artist whose painting moved you, or join an online science club. Over time, these moments knit together, turning strangers into mentors, friends, and collaborators.

Research published in the Journal of Social and Clinical Psychology found that people who use social media for genuine interaction—like exchanging advice or working together on projects—have significantly lower levels of social anxiety and depression than those who just lurk or compare. It's proof: the platform is only as isolating as we let it be.

Connection, real connection, requires showing up as yourself, imperfections and all. If you find a community that celebrates honesty, vulnerability, and effort over image, you'll likely find not just motivation, but real belonging. It's about who's standing beside you, not who's standing out.

Social media doesn't have to be a zero-sum game, where one person's success means another's failure. When we swap comparison for connection, the journey becomes less lonely, and the success of others becomes something to cheer, not fear.

Transforming Envy into Empowerment: Turning Inspiration into Action

We're human; feeling envious sometimes is normal. But what if, instead of letting envy stall us or bruise our self-respect, we let it point us toward what matters most?

Envy can be a powerful indicator. It shines a light on what we desire, what excites us, what we want for ourselves. Noticing a friend's acceptance letter or a peer's performance shouldn't leave us stuck, but stirred up to do more, to dream more. The key is transforming that initial pinch of envy into motivation.

Start with honesty. When envy strikes, admit it to

yourself. Name what you admire. For example, if you're longing for someone else's artistic skills, switch the soundtrack in your mind from "I'll never be that talented" to "I want to improve at this too. Where can I begin?" That shift in language makes a world of difference.

Jay Shetty, former monk and bestselling author, encourages turning envy into curiosity: "Notice what qualities you admire in others. Then ask, how can I cultivate those qualities in my own way, with my own twist?" Shetty's advice echoes research from Stanford University showing that when people set small, specific goals based on what inspires them—rather than vague wishes—they're far more likely to take action and feel happier as a result.

Find a practical next step. If someone's poetry resonates with you, try jotting down lines in your journal tonight. Admire a friend's athleticism? Sign up for a beginner's class or ask them to practice together. Inspiration is only as meaningful as the effort it ignites.

Celebrating others' achievements out loud is also powerful. Tell that friend they did an amazing job or publicly applaud a peer's courage. Compliments are contagious. In classrooms and online, encouragement travels fast, often circling back to you in unexpected ways. When you reflect appreciation instead of resentment, you not only boost someone else's confidence but reinforce your own growth mindset.

The world is wide. There's room for everyone to shine. When we use others' successes as reminders of our own potential, we lift the whole community higher. Little by little, the spark of envy can become the fuel for our boldest dreams.

When you embrace community over comparison, social media transforms from a hall of mirrors into a window—one that lets in more light, fresh perspectives, and the confidence to create a story you're proud to claim. Inspiration is everywhere. Sometimes, you'll find it in the stories of others. Other times, you'll find it in the small choices you make, day after day, to seek connection, not competition. That's where your real power begins.

Chapter 13

Sometimes, the mirror feels like a verdict. You look, searching for what you hope to find—a spark, an acceptance, maybe even a flicker of admiration. But too often, old habits whisper back: you're not enough, you don't fit in, you should be different. These ideas stick, clinging relentlessly, and over time, they shape our sense of worth. But what if you could build something stronger—and truer—inside yourself: a mindset that says not just "I am enough," but "I am worthy, just as I am"?

It starts with a fresh foundation: body positivity that isn't just a trend but a truth woven deep through every thought and action. To truly shift how you feel about your body—and yourself—takes more than a single kind word or a social media post. Real change grows from daily action, reflection, and kindness, practiced again and again. Let's explore how you build that, step by step, and why it has the power to last.

Understanding the Foundations of Body Positivity

Body positivity is talked about everywhere, from

magazine covers to school assemblies. But what is it really? At its core, body positivity is the belief that everyone deserves respect, love, and acceptance—regardless of their physical appearance, size, shape, skin color, or ability.

Research from the National Eating Disorders Association shows that people who practice body positivity report higher self-esteem and a stronger sense of overall wellbeing. They're not immune to challenges, but they rebound faster. They feel more comfortable in their own skin, even on "bad" days.

Dr. Linda Bacon, a leading voice in the Health at Every Size movement, explains, "Body acceptance isn't about pretending you have to love everything every day; it's about recognizing your body as worthy and valuable, no matter what." That distinction matters. Body positivity isn't just about admiring your reflection when it looks "good" but holding space for yourself when it feels hard.

The roots of body positivity stretch back decades to activists who demanded that every body—fat, thin, disabled, scarred, or aging—be given dignity. They challenged beauty standards that said only a narrow few were worthy of love and recognition. Today, those ideas have sparked a global conversation, but cultural standards and everyday pressures can still make it tough to shake self-doubt.

Body positivity is not about pretending hardship

doesn't exist or denying a desire to care for yourself. It's the radical act of showing up for yourself—with courage, patience, and respect—every single day. When these foundations are strong, brighter thoughts and healthier behaviors follow.

Identifying and Challenging Negative Self-Talk

Almost everyone has an inner critic. That voice—it might sound like a parent, a bully, or just a nagging worry—comments on how you look, behave, or measure up. "Why can't you be thinner?" "You shouldn't wear that." "You're not as good as them." These messages, repeated over time, shape your mindset about your body.

Negative self-talk usually begins early, fed by comments from family, media, classmates, and even strangers. Sometimes, you don't even notice the thoughts—they're so quick, like little flashes, that they slide into your head before you can object. Yet left unchecked, these flashes can snowball into full-blown beliefs.

Researchers estimate that the average person has thousands of thoughts every day. According to psychologist Dr. Ethan Kross, up to 80% can be negative, and many revolve around self-criticism or regret. Not all of these are about our bodies, but appearance often takes center stage, especially in adolescence and teen years.

Kylie, a high school junior, shares her story: "I'd walk past a window and instantly look away, just waiting for my mind to pick apart my shape, my clothes, my hair. Sometimes I didn't even realize I was doing it until I felt bad."

The first step to changing this cycle is to notice it in action. Start by tuning in: what do you hear yourself say quietly, or even out loud, about your body on an average day? Do you sigh when you see yourself in photos? Do you shy away from swimming, dancing, or speaking up, afraid someone will judge your appearance? Awareness isn't meant to make you feel guilty, but to give you a clearer picture of where your mindset stands now.

Once you recognize negative self-talk, it's time to challenge it. Ask questions like: Is this thought fair? Would I say this to someone I care about? What evidence do I have that it's even true? Psychologist Dr. Kristin Neff, known for her work on self-compassion, advocates treating yourself as you would a close friend—offering gentleness and understanding instead of scolding.

When you catch yourself thinking something harsh, try pausing and reframing. For example, if you think, "My stomach looks gross," pause. Is that truly helpful or just an old tape playing in your mind? Could you shift to, "My body helps me every day, even when I struggle with how it looks?" This isn't always easy, but repeated often, it changes the script.

Sometimes, you'll need to seek out support. Peer groups, counselors, or community organizations often offer safe spaces to talk about body image. Studies show that discussing negative thoughts, rather than hiding them, helps break their hold over you.

Crafting Personalized Body Positive Affirmations

Words have power. The things you say to yourself, again and again, carve out neural pathways in your brain—much like grooves in a well-worn trail. Over time, those grooves become the path of least resistance; your thoughts tend to follow them without much effort. That's where affirmations come in.

Affirmations are short, positive statements that act like seeds planted in your mind. When these seeds are watered with repetition, they start to sprout and grow roots, changing how you see yourself. Psychologist Dr. Cynthia Belar states, "Affirmations, when authentic and repeated, can begin to restructure negative self-talk and encourage healthier thought patterns."

But here's the key: affirmations need to feel personal and believable, at least a little. You can't go from "I hate my thighs" to "I have the most beautiful legs in the world" and expect it to stick overnight. Instead, affirmations should meet you where you are—and encourage you to shift, step by step.

Start by identifying moments or body parts that spark negative thoughts. Then, look for even a tiny flicker of neutrality or appreciation. Maybe you can't say, "I love my stomach," but perhaps, "My stomach helps me laugh, breathe, and move through life" feels truer. Or "My body deserves kindness, even when I struggle to feel it."

Affirmations might sound like:

- "I am deserving of care, just as I am."
- "My worth is not defined by my appearance."
- "Every day, I choose to treat myself with respect."
- "I appreciate what my body allows me to experience."

Writing your own, in your voice, makes them far more powerful. Try completing sentences like, "Today I honor my body by…" or "I feel proud of my body when…" The more you use your language, the more resonance the words have.

Consistency is important, but variety helps too. Switch up affirmations to match what you need on tough days or when you want to celebrate growth. Repeat them softly in the mirror, jot them in a journal, or even record yourself saying them. Some people place notes on bathroom mirrors or inside notebooks—a visual cue to practice positivity.

If saying affirmations feels awkward at first, you're not

alone. Many people report eye-rolling or self-consciousness during the early days. Over time, though, researchers find that the discomfort fades, replaced by a growing sense of peace. As one college athlete reflected, "I started out rolling my eyes, but six months later, I actually catch myself believing the things I say."

Designing Daily Rituals for Lasting Mindset Shifts

Change doesn't happen in a single afternoon. It builds with tiny, repeated actions—the same way water shapes stone or practice improves a skill. Rituals transform affirmations and positive thinking into habits that are hard to shake, even on difficult days.

A ritual is a set of actions you repeat, often at the same time or in a familiar way. Just like brushing your teeth becomes routine, so can treating yourself with gentleness. The key is making these practices visible and specific, so you know when you're doing them and can track your progress over time.

Morning rituals work for many people. Starting your day with a two-minute affirmation—spoken out loud while you stretch or look in the mirror—sets a positive tone that lingers. Yoga teacher Jessamyn Stanley shares that she begins every morning by thanking her body for carrying her into a new day: "I remind myself that my body is my oldest friend. That small act roots me in gratitude."

Journaling can be another powerful ritual. Each night, write down three things your body allowed you to do. Maybe it's as simple as walking up the stairs or hugging a friend. Over time, these lists become proof that your body is so much more than its appearance.

Movement rituals also support mindset shifts. This doesn't mean forcing yourself through workouts you hate, but moving in joyful ways—a quick dance before dinner, a short stroll, or gentle stretching. When you pair this with positive self-talk ("I am moving to thank my body, not punish it"), exercise becomes an act of celebration.

Some people find music helpful—building playlists of songs that remind them of strength, worth, or happiness. Others use art, drawing self-portraits with kindness, or crafting collages from images that represent body acceptance and hope.

Creating visual reminders, like affirmation cards, sticky notes, or screensavers with encouraging words, can reinforce rituals. Once a month, try writing a letter to your body, expressing gratitude or describing what you've learned.

The key is to start small. Maybe it's one affirmation in the morning, or a gratitude list before bed. As these become natural, add a new ritual or adjust old ones to keep them meaningful.

Importantly, connect your rituals to your real life. If

you struggle with negative thoughts after scrolling through social media, create a ritual: pause, put down your phone, and list three neutral observations about your body. If trying on new clothes is tough, pair it with affirmations or a reward unrelated to size or fit.

It's okay for rituals to change. Some days will be harder than others; you may miss a morning or skip an entry. Kindness matters most: return when you can, and remember that each repetition adds up. Routines, even imperfect ones, shape long-lasting beliefs.

Measuring Progress and Celebrating Self-Growth

Building body confidence isn't like turning on a light switch. There's no clear "before and after." Progress comes in waves—sometimes three steps forward, one step back. What matters most isn't perfection, but persistence and noticing growth, even when it's subtle.

To measure progress, start with reflection. Once a week, take time to notice changes. Can you spot shifts in your daily thoughts, or find it easier to name something you like about yourself? Maybe you reacted differently to a negative comment, spoke up for your needs, or wore something you previously avoided.

Research from the Body Image Movement shows that writing down successes—no matter how small—

reinforces new habits. Gina, an eighth-grader, began tracking moments she caught herself with gentle thoughts: "I used to scribble out photos of myself in group pictures. Now, I pause and look for one thing I like—my smile or the color of my shirt. It sounds silly, but it helps."

Setbacks are natural. There will be days when old voices creep back in, or when outside pressures make everything feel impossible. Note these too, without criticism. Each "hard" day offers insight about which situations trigger negative thinking, and helps you prepare for next time.

Celebrating self-growth means noticing every victory. Maybe it's a week of saying affirmations without rolling your eyes, or dancing without comparing yourself to others. Maybe it's simply wearing shorts on a hot day, without covering up, or joining a group activity you'd normally avoid.

Don't wait for giant milestones. Dr. Rashmi Parmar, a psychiatrist specializing in youth mental health, says, "We often overlook small improvements, but it's those micro-moments—standing a bit taller, speaking a bit kinder—that signal genuine healing and growth." Reward yourself for these: with a movie night, a new journal, time with friends, or anything that feels nourishing.

Sharing progress with someone you trust can magnify its impact. Call a friend, text a family member, or talk with a mentor. Celebrating together turns personal victories into collective joy, showing that body positivity isn't a journey made in isolation.

If you keep a journal or vision board, look back over older entries every month or two. You'll often be surprised at how much your thoughts and feelings have shifted, even if it's not always obvious in the moment.

Everyone grows at their own pace. Comparison drains joy; gratitude fills it. Measuring progress isn't about getting to a perfect place, but about noticing how you're moving towards kindness—step by step, moment by moment.

As your sense of acceptance expands and rituals deepen, affirmations become second nature. One day, you may catch yourself helping a friend through their own struggles, passing along what you've learned. That's the true gift of building a body positive mindset: not just healing yourself, but helping to create a world where everyone knows they belong.

Chapter 14

Saying yes to yourself can be surprisingly hard. It sounds simple enough. Who wouldn't want to put themselves first sometimes? But the truth is, for a lot of people, just the idea stirs up feelings of guilt, selfishness, or even fear. We're taught, often from a young age, to care for others, to pitch in, to share — all noble values. Yet somewhere between sharing our toys as kids and sharing the emotional labor as adults, many of us forget to share care with ourselves. That's why self-care is actually a much bigger deal, a much more radical act, than the face masks and bubble baths that show up on social media.

That's where the shift begins.

Redefining Self-Care: Moving Beyond Superficial Acts

If you look up "self-care" online, you're met with a sea of glossy images: bath bombs fizzing in tubs, scented candles flickering, beautiful journals open to blank pages. While there's nothing wrong with these things, sometimes these images make self-care seem frivolous. Or they suggest that spending money on products is the answer to feeling better.

Real self-care, though, is much bigger than that.

True self-care asks us to tend to ourselves — not just on weekends, or during a spa day, but in all the small, everyday moments when we matter. It asks us to notice what drains us and what fills us up. Sometimes, self-care is about saying "no" even when you fear disappointing someone. Sometimes, it's reaching out for help during a rough patch, or recognizing that an extra hour of sleep is more healing than binge-watching a show.

Bestselling author and therapist Nedra Glover Tawwab reminds us, "Self-care isn't selfish. It's essential." This means realizing that taking care of yourself doesn't take away from anyone else. In fact, tending to your own needs puts you in a stronger position to support others.

And there's another side to this: self-care that matters isn't always pretty. Sometimes it's having that hard conversation you've put off for weeks. Sometimes it's scheduling a doctor's appointment you've been avoiding. Other times, it's letting yourself grieve, rest, or express anger without judgment.

Self-care is also about boundaries — noticing when your energy or emotions are running low, and protecting yourself from what drains you. It's about tuning in to your real needs, the ones under the surface.

So the next time you see an ad promising happiness in a bottle, pause and ask yourself: what do I really need right now? The answer might surprise you.

Understanding Self-Love as an Act of Defiance

Self-love can feel rebellious, even bold. That's because we live in a world where many messages remind us to shrink ourselves, to hustle harder, to never be satisfied. Buying into those messages can make self-criticism and self-denial feel normal, like they're just part of being "motivated" or "disciplined."

But what happens when you start saying yes to yourself on purpose?

When you decide you are worthy of kindness, respect, rest, and compassion, you're breaking the quiet rules that say only certain people deserve care. You're standing up to a culture that profits from your insecurity. And you're claiming your right to joy — not just survival.

Audre Lorde, the legendary poet and activist, wrote, "Caring for myself is not self-indulgence, it is self-preservation, and that is an act of political warfare." Those are powerful words. Lorde reminds us that self-love can be a radical act, especially for people who have been told in big or small ways that they're not enough. Every time you choose self-love, you push back on systems, traditions, or beliefs that say you don't deserve it.

There's data to back this up. Studies from the University of Texas found that higher self-compassion leads to lower anxiety, greater resilience, and even physical health benefits. When you treat yourself with gentleness and respect, you build up reserves of strength that help you face both daily stress and bigger life challenges.

It might seem easier to just go along with the grind, to keep your head down and ignore your needs. But saying yes to yourself — especially in small, everyday ways — rewires your brain to expect kindness, not just from others, but from within. It's defiance wrapped in softness, a quiet stand you take every day.

Identifying and Challenging Internalized Barriers to Self-Care

You might notice resistance bubbling up as you try to put your own needs first. Maybe you hear an inner voice that says, "You don't deserve to rest until you finish everything." Or perhaps a pang of guilt shows up when you cancel plans that would stretch you too thin.

These reactions aren't random; they're shaped by family upbringing, culture, even the media you consume. For example, if your parents or caregivers put everyone else's needs before their own, you may have learned to do the same. Or, if you grew up hearing that hard work is the only path to worthiness, taking breaks may stir up anxiety.

Dr. Kristin Neff, one of the leading researchers on self-compassion, explains, "We often believe that self-criticism is necessary for self-improvement. But in truth, self-compassion — not harshness — is what drives us forward in a healthy way." The idea that we have to earn care, even from ourselves, is one that needs questioning.

Start by becoming aware of your internal dialogue. Notice what phrases pop up when you try to rest or ask for help. Are you hearing someone else's words in your mind? Old messages from childhood, perhaps, or echoes of teachers, bosses, or social media influencers? Sometimes, just noticing these thoughts is enough to loosen their grip.

Another barrier is fear: fear of missing out, fear of being seen as lazy, fear of not being enough. These emotions are normal, but it's worth asking yourself where they come from and whether they're really telling you the truth.

Write these thoughts down. Challenge them gently. Would you speak the same way to someone you love? If not, it might be time to rewrite the script.

For some, cultural or societal expectations set thick, almost invisible barriers. If you come from a background where sacrifice is prized — maybe as a sign of love or character — self-care can feel unnatural or even wrong. Research from the National Alliance on Mental Illness shows that people facing these barriers report higher rates of burnout and stress, especially when they don't feel free to call a timeout.

But options exist. You can respect the traditions that shaped you and still choose to carve out room for yourself. Even five minutes, taken just for you, is a start.

Developing a Personalized Self-Care Practice Rooted in Self-Compassion

Now comes the creative part: what does caring for yourself really look like, for you?

There's no one-size-fits-all answer. For one person, self-care might mean starting each morning with a quiet cup of tea. For another, it might mean joining a pick-up basketball game, or spending time laughing with friends, or journaling before bed.

The difference between self-care and simple reward is intention. Are you doing this to truly nurture yourself, or to escape? The best self-care routines are rooted in self-compassion — a genuine belief that you are worthy of kindness, especially from yourself.

Ask yourself: When do I feel most at ease? Most energized? Most peaceful? Think back on what used to delight you as a child. Maybe you loved drawing, or building forts, or looking at the stars. Those core joys don't just fade away — they wait patiently beneath the surface.

Try making a list of the activities that feed you. Be as specific as you can. Instead of "exercise," write "dancing to old pop songs for fifteen minutes." Instead of "rest," write "lying in a hammock under the tree in the backyard."

Track what feels nourishing. Some days, watching a favorite show is truly restorative. Other days, it might be moving your body or connecting with a friend who always lifts you up. In her book "The Gifts of Imperfection," researcher Brené Brown describes how self-care is a "practice" — something you return to, experiment with, and revise over time.

It helps to have different kinds of care on your menu. What do you need when you're physically tired? Emotionally worn out? Spiritually low? As you get to know yourself better, your menu of self-care options will become richer and more satisfying.

Compassion is key. Sometimes, even with the best intentions, you'll skip your self-care rituals. Life gets busy. That's not a reason for self-blame. If you forget yourself for a while, the answer isn't punishment — it's permission to begin again.

Cultivating Consistency: Integrating Radical Self-Love

into Daily Life

So how does self-care, and the deeper self-love beneath it, become a regular part of life instead of an occasional treat?

The answer is commitment, not perfection. Too often, self-care is framed as something you "earn" after a hard week — a rare treat, tucked in among obligations. But you deserve attention every single day, not just after you're depleted.

Small routines matter. Instead of waiting for stress levels to rise, sprinkle moments of care throughout your day. Maybe you stretch for a few minutes between meetings, pause to breathe deeply when you notice your shoulders tensing, or unplug from screens instead of scrolling through social media right before bed.

Research from Stanford University shows that micro-habits — tiny, consistent actions — are much more likely to stick than giant changes made all at once. The simple act of checking in with yourself at regular intervals opens space for self-compassion to grow. It's like watering a plant; the growth is slow, but steady.

Accountability helps too. Share your self-care goals with a friend or family member who believes you matter. Let them cheer you on, or even join you in your routine. Witnessing someone else's journey of self-love can reinforce your own.

Remind yourself why self-care is vital. When you treat yourself well, you're not only honoring your own needs — you're modeling to others that kindness begins at home. You won't be perfect, and you don't have to be. It's the returning, again and again, that makes the difference.

Many people find visual cues helpful: a note on your mirror, a phone reminder, or a meaningful bracelet you wear as a signal to check in with yourself. Others like to celebrate the small wins — noticing when they chose to rest instead of power through, or when they reached for comfort without apology.

In time, radical self-love becomes less about doing certain things and more about seeing yourself with soft eyes. You grow accustomed to gentle words and patient practices. You expect warmth from yourself. That's not arrogance; it's the baseline you need to thrive.

Integrating self-love into your life won't solve all problems or erase every difficulty — but it changes how you move through them. It changes the kinds of boundaries you set and the ones you honor. You become both softer and stronger, a blend as potent as anything in nature.

Remember, saying yes to yourself doesn't mean saying no to everyone else. It simply means you've decided that your well-being is non-negotiable.

When you show up for yourself, day after steady day, you create a ripple effect of care that touches every part of your world.

What would it feel like to make self-love your habit, not just your hope? The answer, lived out in small, daily choices, can shift your entire sense of what's possible.

Chapter 15

Have you ever walked into a classroom, work meeting, or a new friend group and felt like you had to adjust yourself—just a bit—to fit in? Maybe you laughed at a joke that didn't feel funny to you or said yes to something you didn't really want. Most of us have had those moments. They can leave us feeling uneasy or as if we're wearing someone else's shoes. But there's another way to approach the world: leading with confidence by showing up as your genuine self—authentically, every time.

Authenticity isn't just a nice idea; it's a living, breathing necessity for healthy confidence. But what exactly does it mean to "show up as yourself"? Is it about being bold all the time? Does it mean you share everything, everywhere? The truth is much more nuanced, and understanding it is the foundation of genuine confidence.

Understanding Authenticity: What It Means to Show Up as Yourself

Authenticity means living in a way that's true to who you really are—your thoughts, feelings, beliefs, and values. It's the quiet strength you feel when your inside matches your outside. Imagine someone who truly enjoys painting. When they speak about art, their eyes light up, their words flow easily, and the passion is obvious. They're showing up authentically, even if some people around them aren't interested in art.

Dr. Brené Brown, a researcher who has spent decades studying vulnerability and courage, defines authenticity as "the daily practice of letting go of who we think we're supposed to be and embracing who we are." This doesn't mean ignoring social cues or disregarding others' feelings. Instead, it's about honoring your own truth while respecting the world around you.

Picture yourself at a friend's birthday party. Everyone's dancing and you're not a fan of dancing in public. Being authentic might mean allowing yourself to stay on the sidelines, clap along, and enjoy the music without forcing yourself onto the dance floor just because "everyone else is doing it." Over time, small choices like this help you build an internal compass—one that points firmly to your own north, not someone else's map.

Authenticity also doesn't mean oversharing—blurting out every thought or detail about your life isn't required. It's more about honesty, clarity, and alignment between your inner and outer worlds. Others can sense authenticity. There's an openness to authentic people, a feeling that you're seeing the real person rather than a mask. This draws people in and builds trust.

Identifying and Overcoming Barriers to Authentic Self-Expression

So, if authenticity is so rewarding, why does it feel so hard at times? A big piece of the puzzle lies in the barriers that block us—often, these don't even come from outside us, but from within.

Fear is perhaps the largest wall we hit. The fear of being judged, misunderstood, or flat-out rejected sticks with us. It might have started in small ways, maybe even as far back as childhood with an embarrassing moment or an unkind comment. As we grow, those moments can get stored away like pebbles in our shoes—annoying, but not enough to make us stop. Over time, without noticing, they can start to change our walk.

Social pressure is powerful, too. Psychologists call it "social conformity." It's a human instinct to want to belong to a group, and blending in feels safe. However, as writer Oscar Wilde famously quipped, "Be yourself; everyone else is already taken." When we conform too much, we lose touch with what makes us unique.

Cultural or familial expectations are shaped by where and how you grew up. Perhaps your family carries generations of beliefs about the "right" way to behave or choose a path. Breaking away from those can feel like betraying your roots, even angering those you care about. This tension makes it challenging to bring your true self forward.

There are more subtle barriers, too. Habits like perfectionism—wanting to do or say only what's "acceptable"—can trap you in cycles of overthinking and self-editing. Perfectionism seems helpful but often ends up paralyzing. Researcher Dr. Kristin Neff notes that self-compassion—treating yourself kindly, especially when you make mistakes—can short-circuit perfectionist thinking and help you see yourself more clearly.

Yet another obstacle is comparison. That voice inside that whispers, "They're smarter, cooler, more talented"—that's the thief of joy, as Theodore Roosevelt so bluntly put it. Social media amplifies this, making it look like everyone else has it figured out. But remember, you're seeing highlight reels, not the whole story.

Whatever the barrier, recognizing it is the first powerful move you can make. Becoming aware of what's holding you back is like catching a trickster red-handed in your own mind. This opens the door to change.

Cultivating Self-Awareness to Strengthen Confidence

Getting to know yourself is the beating heart of authenticity. Self-awareness is being able to notice your thoughts, feelings, and behaviors—not just in quiet moments, but in action, right when things get tough.

Why does self-awareness matter so much? Studies from Harvard Business Review show that people who understand their thoughts, emotions, and motives are more confident and perform better, both personally and professionally. When you know who you are, your confidence grows from the inside—less shaken by what others think or say because you trust your own motives.

One helpful approach is reflection. It's not just about thinking deeply, but pausing and taking time to check in with yourself. Journaling works wonders for this. A simple prompt like, "What mattered most to me today?" or "When did I feel most myself?" can uncover patterns in your reactions, desires, and fears.

Listening to feedback, both from yourself and trusted allies, is another tool. This doesn't mean accepting every criticism, but being open to learning about blindspots or places where you might fall into old patterns. Sometimes we wear masks we don't even realize are there until someone gently points it out.

Mindfulness—the practice of noticing what's happening right now, without harsh judgment—provides another path toward self-awareness. Even a few minutes a day of breathing, walking outdoors, or listening quietly can help you tune into signals your body and mind send. Dr. Jon Kabat-Zinn, known for bringing mindfulness into modern medicine, suggests that "you can't stop the waves, but you can learn to surf." The more you practice, the easier it becomes to notice when you're drifting away from your authentic self, and gently course-correct.

Don't forget that self-awareness includes celebrating your unique qualities, not just noticing what needs work. Confidence comes from recognizing your strengths and values. Maybe your sense of humor brightens people's days, or your patience builds trust. List these out—yes, actually write them down. Seeing them manifested in words helps build the backbone of steady self-belief.

Practical Strategies for Bringing Your True Self into Different Settings

So, you've understood what authenticity is and what can get in the way. Now, how does this translate into real life? Because, let's be honest, theory only goes so far—what about the awkward family dinner? Or the group project where everyone seems louder than you? Or an interview where you're desperate to make a good impression?

Start with small acts. You don't have to overhaul your whole personality overnight. Practice sharing your honest opinions on topics that matter to you, even if that means gently disagreeing. The trick is to focus on the message, not the volume. For example, if friends want to watch a scary movie and it's not your thing, you might say, "I'd love to hang out, but scary movies really aren't for me. I'll join next time." You're not criticizing the group, just expressing yourself with respect.

Setting boundaries is another vital strategy. Boundaries are like invisible fences that keep you feeling safe, respected, and authentic. They allow you to say "no" when something doesn't align with your values or needs, without guilt. Dr. Henry Cloud, an expert on personal growth, says, "Boundaries define us. They define what is me and what is not me." For example, if your own downtime is important, it's okay to turn down invitations sometimes.

Adapt your authenticity to the context, not your worth. This means you can share different sides of yourself depending on where you are—your sense of humor might shine with friends, while your curiosity leads the way at school or work. This isn't being fake, it's being flexible. Think of it like tuning a guitar: you're still the same instrument, but you adjust the strings based on the song.

Preparation is your ally, especially in new or stressful situations. Before an important conversation or event, remind yourself of your values and strengths. Visualize responding as your best self, not just reacting. Some people find it helpful to practice what they want to say, or even write it down first. This doesn't script your life, but it gives your authentic voice a place to start.

Pay attention to the people and places where you feel safest and most "you." What's different there? Who are you with? How does your body feel? Knowing your "authentic comfort zones" gives you a base to return to when you need to recharge. Over time, with practice, you'll find it easier to bring that true self into less familiar spaces.

And remember, authenticity connects. Consider the story of Sam, a shy student who loved poetry but was afraid to share it. When Sam finally read a poem aloud in class, the nerves were sky-high. But as the words flowed, something remarkable happened—the room grew quiet, classmates leaned in, and afterwards, several others shared their own secret passions. One person's authentic act opened the door for many more.

Maintaining Authenticity in the Face of Judgment or Rejection

Even with preparation, living out your authenticity isn't without bumps. Sometimes, it's uncomfortable. There will be people who don't understand, who judge, who maybe even push back or reject you. This is where the rubber meets the road for confidence. So what do you do when being yourself feels risky?

First, remind yourself that judgment is part of life. Psychologist Dr. Carol Dweck, known for her work on mindset, points out that resilience—the ability to bounce back—grows every time you face challenge and don't shrink from it. "Becoming is better than being," she writes, emphasizing the strength in growing more authentic, even when it's hard.

It helps to shrink the spotlight in your mind. Humans have what scientists call the "spotlight effect"—we overestimate how intensely others notice us. In reality, people are usually too busy worrying about their own stuff to focus on yours. If someone rejects or criticizes your authentic self, that says more about their preferences than your worth.

Build a support system—a few trusted people who get the real you. These might be family members, old friends, a mentor, or even an online community of like-minded souls. When judgment stings, their words can remind you, "You belong. You matter."

Consider feedback, but don't let it define you. Sometimes, criticism can be constructive—it offers a chance to learn. At other times, it's just noise. The art is in telling the difference. If someone attacks your values, style, or dreams and offers nothing useful in return, their feedback isn't worth your energy.

Above all, practice self-compassion. Acknowledge the ache of rejection or the sting of sideways glances. Remind yourself, as Dr. Neff suggests, that imperfection is part of being human. Mistakes and missteps don't erase your value—they're proof that you're living and learning.

Cultivating authenticity is a lifelong journey, one that's rarely linear. Some days, you might feel invincible in your own skin. Other days, doubt sneaks in, and you feel tempted to hide parts of yourself. The rhythm of confidence lies not in perfection, but in returning to yourself again and again.

Each time you choose your real voice, your unfiltered laugh, your honest "no," you lay another brick in the house of your self-esteem. Every moment is an opportunity to practice—and as with all things, practice makes you stronger. The more you show up authentically, the more confident and connected you'll feel, wherever your journey leads.

Chapter 16

Boundaries and desires shape the foundation of every relationship. They define what makes us comfortable, what lights us up, and what helps us feel safe with another person. Without them, we run the risk of losing ourselves—of drifting into situations that don't feel quite right or of agreeing to things that we wish we hadn't. When two people come together, each brings their own unique set of needs, hopes, and limits. The magic, and sometimes the challenge, is sharing those inner realities in a way that creates connection rather than distance.

Everyone experiences boundaries and desires differently. For Maya, a high school sophomore, her boundaries meant saying no to sharing her social media passwords with her boyfriend, even though most of her friends thought it was a normal thing to do. For Juan, it meant asking for time to himself after school before texting anyone, allowing his mind to decompress. These stories are as different as each person reading them, yet they highlight a universal truth—every healthy relationship relies on understanding yourself and being brave enough to express what you truly need.

Understanding Personal Boundaries and Desires

Boundaries aren't walls. They're more like fences with gates—structures we put in place to protect our emotional, mental, and physical wellbeing, while still allowing for closeness and connection. Think of your boundaries as the rules or guidelines that help you feel respected and secure. Desires, on the other hand, are the things that bring us joy, excitement, or fulfillment within relationships. Sometimes, boundaries and desires overlap; sometimes, they pull in different directions.

Recognizing your own boundaries takes time. Maybe you've been in a situation that left you feeling uneasy—a friend joked about something personal, or a partner wanted to move faster than you felt comfortable. Those uneasy feelings are clues. Dr. Brené Brown, a well-respected researcher in the field of empathy and vulnerability, once said, "Daring to set boundaries is about having the courage to love ourselves, even when we risk disappointing others." When you notice anger, resentment, or discomfort rising up, it's a sign your boundaries might need some adjusting.

Desires are just as important. They might include a need for physical affection, quality time, privacy, or even freedom to spend time with friends. Sometimes, people feel ashamed or guilty about what they want, believing their desires aren't valid. But psychologist

Dr. Esther Perel emphasizes that "Desire thrives in freedom and honesty. It dies in secrecy and self-denial." Acknowledging what makes you happy—and sharing that with your partner—boosts trust and intimacy.

Part of understanding your boundaries and desires means reflecting on your experiences, both good and bad. Take a moment to remember a time when you felt especially comfortable with someone. What was happening? What did they say or do that made you feel understood? Or, if it's easier, think back to a time that made you uncomfortable. Were your needs ignored? Did you feel pressured? These memories offer valuable insights into where your boundaries naturally lie.

Identifying and Articulating Your Needs

Once you tune into your boundaries and desires, expressing them is the next step. This can be hard. Nerves might flutter in your chest, or your thoughts might tumble around and refuse to settle. That's completely normal. Many people worry about upsetting their partner or being seen as "difficult." But holding in your needs isn't just unfair to you—it can also harm the relationship by creating confusion or resentment.

To start, try to be specific about what you need and why it matters. Instead of saying, "I don't like it when you text me a lot," you might say, "I get overwhelmed when my phone is buzzing constantly. I'd really appreciate having some quiet time in the evenings." This frames your boundary as something personal, not a criticism of the other person. Using "I" statements rather than "you" statements shifts the focus away from blame and toward understanding.

An example can make this clearer. Consider Leo, who feels uneasy when his girlfriend hugs or kisses him in front of large groups. Rather than snapping, "Stop being so clingy," he takes a breath and says, "I love spending time with you, but I feel nervous with a lot of PDA. Can we show affection more privately?" This kind of honest, direct communication creates space for both people's feelings.

Experts agree on the power of clear communication. Dr. Marshall Rosenberg, creator of Nonviolent Communication, points out that "what others do may be the stimulus of our feelings, but not the cause." In other words, it's okay to tell someone what matters to you without making them responsible for your emotions. The point isn't to control their behavior, but to invite them into a partnership where both voices are heard.

Journaling can help clarify what you want to say. Sometimes, the words flow more easily on paper before they come out in conversation. You might even role-play the conversation with a trusted friend or family member. The main thing is to practice. The more you express your needs, the easier it becomes—

and the more natural it feels.

Active Listening and Mutual Respect in Conversations

Communication is a two-way street. It's not just about saying what you need but truly hearing your partner when they express themselves. Active listening means giving your full attention—not planning a rebuttal or scrolling your phone, but really focusing on the words, the tone, even the body language. It shows your partner that their feelings matter, that they aren't alone.

Research backs this up. Studies from the Gottman Institute—a leading relationship research center—show that couples who regularly practice active listening report greater satisfaction and lower rates of conflict. The act of being listened to, without judgment or interruption, can diffuse tension almost immediately.

Emma, seventeen, remembers a time when her boyfriend told her he felt left out when she went to parties without inviting him. At first, she felt criticized. But then, she listened—really listened—and realized he wasn't angry, just worried about feeling excluded. That moment completely changed the direction of their conversation. She acknowledged his feelings, explained her need for occasional solo time, and together they found a compromise.

Mutual respect underlies these conversations. It's

easy to react defensively when confronted with a boundary you don't like or a desire you don't share. But respect means honoring your partner's feelings, even when you don't agree with them. It means not pushing someone past their comfort zone or rolling your eyes at what they say.

Dr. John Gottman calls this "turning toward" rather than "turning away." When someone reaches out with a need or concern, you have a choice—to engage with curiosity and respect, or to shut them down. That simple difference—how you respond in those everyday moments—often determines the strength and happiness of the relationship over time.

Body language matters here, too. Nodding, making eye contact, and leaning in while your partner talks all show that you're engaged. Try paraphrasing what you've heard: "So, you feel stressed when I do X—is that right?" This gives your partner a chance to clarify or correct any misunderstandings and deepens your connection.

Managing Disagreements and Setting Limits

No matter how much two people care about each other, disagreements will happen. Sometimes, setting a boundary or expressing a desire can spark hurt feelings or even conflict. This isn't a sign that the relationship is doomed—it's a natural part of being human. The key is to handle disagreements with empathy and a willingness to find common ground.

In the heat of a disagreement, our fight-or-flight response often kicks in. Voices rise, tempers flare, and it can feel like the only way forward is for someone to "win." But effective conflict resolution is about understanding, not defeating, each other. Nearly every relationship expert—Sue Johnson, Terrence Real, and others—highlight that managing disagreements well is about setting limits respectfully and acknowledging both people's needs.

Consider this example: Taylor prefers texting over phone calls, while Sam finds texting impersonal and wants nightly calls. Instead of arguing over who's right, they talk about what each style means to them. Taylor feels anxious talking on the phone after a long day—her social battery runs low. Sam feels connected hearing Taylor's voice, especially since they can't see each other in person often. With honest communication, they settle on a few short calls each week, blending both their needs.

Boundaries during disagreements are especially important. Maybe one person needs to take a break and cool off before continuing the discussion. Saying, "I need fifteen minutes to calm down, and then we can talk," isn't a rejection—it's a way of honoring both your limit and your partner's need for resolution. Setting limits can also sound like, "I don't feel comfortable with the way we're talking right now. Can we try speaking more calmly?" While this might feel awkward or even risky at first, it helps steer the conversation toward something healthier.

If disagreements start to go in circles, it sometimes helps to bring in an outside perspective. Family, friends, or even a counselor can provide neutral ground. A 2020 study from the Journal of Family Psychology found that couples who sought outside support during persistent communication struggles were three times more likely to report feeling "heard and understood" months later.

It's also important to forgive mistakes—your partner's and your own. There will be times when someone says the wrong thing or pushes a boundary unintentionally. Relationships thrive when both people are willing to apologize, make amends, and adjust their behavior moving forward.

Building Ongoing Communication Habits with Partners

Open and honest communication isn't something you do just once. It's a skill that grows with practice—a habit woven into the fabric of your days, both big and small. Strong relationships don't just happen; they're built on regular check-ins, honest conversations, and a shared willingness to nurture trust.

Many couples have simple rituals that keep the lines of communication open. This might be as easy as asking, "How are you feeling about us?" once a week.

Or, for some, it's a nightly habit of sharing one good thing and one hard thing from your day. It doesn't have to be formal or serious every time; laughter, storytelling, and playfulness can be just as important as the deep talks.

Researchers at UCLA found that couples who frequently "update" each other about their feelings and boundaries—sometimes called "state of the union" talks—experience less stress and more intimacy than those who only talk when problems arise. These conversations allow for small adjustments before issues pile up and become overwhelming.

Trust is the core ingredient. Without it, even the best communication techniques fall flat. Trust is built in a hundred small ways—keeping promises, showing up when you say you will, respecting each other's privacy, and giving each other the benefit of the doubt. When trust is present, both people feel safer sharing their truest selves.

There's also value in celebrating each other's boundaries and desires. When you notice your partner taking care of themselves or expressing a need with courage, acknowledge it. Saying, "I appreciate you telling me how you feel," or "Thanks for trusting me with that," signals your commitment to their comfort. Dr. Gary Chapman, author of The Five Love Languages, explains this as "speaking each other's language"—figuring out not just what is said, but what is felt beneath the words.

Flexibility plays a big role too. What worked last month might not work now. People change, schedules adjust, new pressures appear, and old discomforts fade away. Make it a regular habit to check in about boundaries and desires, knowing that the answers might shift with time. This ongoing curiosity is what keeps a relationship alive and growing.

Sometimes communication breaks down. Maybe something goes unsaid for too long, or an old argument creeps back in. When that happens, it can help to return to the basics: listen with empathy, speak honestly, and assume your partner's good intentions. Most conflicts have less to do with the specific issue and more to do with feeling unheard or misunderstood.

As you build these habits, you'll likely notice that disagreements become easier to navigate, desires feel safer to express, and boundaries come to be seen not as obstacles but as invitations—to know yourself better, to trust your partner deeply, and to share a connection that is honest, resilient, and real.

The heart of any meaningful connection is found in these everyday acts of sharing—small admissions of what makes us feel right, moments of attentive listening, gifts of courage as we voice a difficult need. Through the seasons of silence and the afternoons filled with animated laughter, it's the steady conversation—sometimes loud, sometimes quiet—that shapes the path forward together. In the gentle work of speaking up and hearing each other, two people become, not perfect, but beautifully understood.

Chapter 17

In the last ten years, the word "body positivity" has exploded online. Suddenly, social media is full of people of all different shapes, sizes, and backgrounds proudly sharing images of themselves, sometimes in clothes society didn't think they "should" wear, sometimes without filters or fancy lighting at all. But body positivity didn't start on Instagram or TikTok. Its roots stretch back decades, born from people—often marginalized themselves—rejecting the tired notion that only certain bodies are good enough.

What's different now is the tremendous platform social media provides. Before, the world saw only a narrow range of appearances in magazines, billboards, and movies—most often white, thin, able-bodied people. Now, people everywhere can share their own truths. Anyone can become a symbol of self-acceptance for thousands or even millions of followers, right from their bedroom. And more than ever, young people are growing up seeing bodies like their own celebrated on their screens.

Defining Body Positivity in the Social Media Era

Body positivity means different things to different people, but at its heart, it's a movement aimed at respecting and loving your body, just as it is, at every size and stage of life. In this social media age, body positivity encourages rejecting unrealistic beauty standards. It's about appreciating what your body does for you, focusing on health and happiness over appearance, and recognizing that worth isn't dependent on weight, shape, or skin color.

Social media added a fast-moving current to this cause. Instagram, TikTok, Twitter, and YouTube have become megaphones for people who, for generations, felt invisible. They're not just showing bodies of every variety—they're celebrating stretch marks, scars, disability, aging, and the changes that come with puberty or illness. Where once only carefully curated, idealized images appeared in public, now the curtain is getting pulled back—sometimes in joyful, messy, and totally unfiltered ways.

But like any trend, body positivity can be misunderstood. For some, it becomes a branding exercise, a set of hashtags attached to flawless selfies. Others mistake it for promoting unhealthy habits or ignore the intersectional roots of the movement—that is, the ways body acceptance is influenced by race, gender, disability, sexuality, and culture. True body positivity isn't just about posting bikini photos with a clever caption. It's about challenging the systems that tell us only some people are deserving of confidence and care.

In one interview, Dr. Rachel Goldman, a psychologist specializing in body image, explained, "Social media has democratized representation. More people see themselves reflected, and that visibility is powerful. Still, it matters that we understand body positivity as something deeper than trends or likes."

Spotlight on Influencers: Diverse Voices and Lived Experiences

Behind those hashtags are real people, each with their own story—a fierce teenager recovering from an eating disorder, a mother navigating stretch marks after childbirth, a wheelchair user fighting for accessible fashion, or someone in transition affirming their gender and body. The faces of body positivity on social media aren't all the same, and that's exactly the point.

Take Lizzo, for example. Superstar, singer, flutist, and unapologetic champion of self-love, Lizzo has shattered stereotypes about who gets to feel sexy, strong, and unstoppable. When tabloids criticized her fashion choices, she replied with laughter and a new single—or a bold dance video for her millions of followers. For many young fans, Lizzo's confidence is a gentle (and sometimes very loud) reminder: joy is not reserved for the thin, the white, the traditionally "pretty."

In another corner of Instagram, Jessica Kellgren-Fozard, a British creator with chronic illnesses, uses her platform to bust myths about disability. She brings humor, vintage style, and plenty of honesty, making her followers feel seen—not in spite of her differences, but because of them. "Disability is just another way of being human," she once wrote in a post that received thousands of supportive comments.

Then there's Nabela Noor, a Bangladeshi-American beauty influencer, who grew up doubting whether her body and skin tone were "good enough"—until she realized her lived experience was exactly what the beauty world needed. Through makeup tutorials and candid conversations, Nabela teaches her followers to stop shrinking themselves, literally and figuratively. In one viral reel, she shared: "We do not need to get smaller to make more space for others. Let's take up all the space we need."

One of the most impactful parts of following body positive influencers is seeing how much diversity is possible—not just in bodies, but in journeys. Some people share tips for managing acne or vitiligo. Others tell stories of gender affirmation, or learning to embrace natural hair despite years of being told to "tame" it. The mosaic grows richer with every new voice.

These influencers bridge a gap between the old world of flawless, touch-up-magazine ads and the real world most people live in. Their posts are more than just pretty pictures. They're proof that worth can't be measured by a scale, isn't limited by a wheelchair, and doesn't fade after age twenty-nine. The most powerful stories online are the ones that dare to be honest—even when the world isn't always kind in return.

Breaking Myths: What Authentic Body Positivity Looks Like

As the movement gathers followers—and critics—it's important to clear up what body positivity really does and doesn't mean.

First, it doesn't mean pretending to love every single thing about your body every day. Even the most celebrated influencers talk openly about bad days and insecurities. Megan Crabbe, author and creator behind "BodyPosiPanda," has said, "Self-love isn't a destination. It's a practice." She often revisits the story of her eating disorder recovery—not to glamorize the struggle, but to remind others that healing comes in waves.

Next, true body positivity isn't about ignoring health. Many critics argue that celebrating bigger bodies encourages unhealthy lifestyles, but experts push back. As nutritionist Christy Harrison points out, "Health isn't a look—it's a set of behaviors." A person's physical and emotional health can't be determined just by looking at their size. What's truly radical about body positivity is its insistence that everyone deserves respect and care—regardless of weight, ability, skin, or scars.

Rather than urging people to love themselves only when they fit a certain mold, authentic body positivity stands up to the endless rules set by culture, fashion, and advertising. It says, "You do not have to earn your right to like yourself." In a post that struck a chord with thousands, influencer Stephanie Yeboah shared, "Growing up, every store I walked into told me I did not belong. Every magazine cover told me love was for later—maybe never. I am done waiting for someone to choose me."

Authentic body positivity also doesn't mean rejecting self-improvement. Some think the movement asks people to abandon fitness, grooming, or the desire to change. In reality, most influencers emphasize that if someone wants to exercise, dress up, or eat nutritiously, these things should come from a place of care—not self-punishment. Body positivity lets people ask, "What feels good for me?" instead of "What will help me shrink?"

Perhaps most important, real body positivity understands the difference between positivity and toxic positivity. It welcomes sadness, frustration, and grief. After all, it's not always easy to unlearn the lessons taught by decades of harmful messaging. "It's normal to struggle with your body sometimes," therapist Sonya Renee Taylor reminds her followers.

"What matters is how you talk to yourself on the hard days."

Navigating Social Media: Balancing Inspiration with Reality

While influencers can be inspiring, the social media world isn't always friendly. Like any tool, these apps can be helpful or harmful, depending on how they're used. It's easy to compare ourselves to others—especially when scrolling through picture-perfect feeds. Yet underneath the filters and clever edits, everyone has struggles you can't see in a square photo.

Harvard's Center on Media and Child Health found that young people who spent more time curating their selfie posts or comparing their bodies to influencers reported more body dissatisfaction. Even when following supposedly "body positive" accounts, it's possible to feel less worthy if the underlying message is still about looking a certain way.

So, what helps? It starts with following people who make you feel seen, not small. Seek out pages that celebrate bodies who look—well, like yours! There's no shame in unfollowing or muting accounts that make you anxious or critical, even if they're popular. Your feed should fuel your joy and curiosity, not feed insecurity.

It's also important to remember that everyone

curates their social feed. Influencers, too, aren't showing every moment of self-doubt or struggle. When model Iskra Lawrence admitted to breaking down in tears before a shoot, her followers were reminded that nobody is happy 100% of the time—not even the ones paid to smile.

Reality checks are healthy. Remind yourself that cellulite, acne, scars, and weight fluctuations are normal. Everyone is at a different place in their journey to self-acceptance. If an influencer shares their "before and after," remember it's likely not the whole story. Growth, healing, and confidence aren't always visible on camera.

Another tricky trend is "body positivity" being co-opted by brands and advertisers. Sometimes, companies use the vocabulary of self-love just to sell more product—without truly supporting the values behind the movement. That's why so many real influencers go out of their way to call out empty slogans and demand actual diversity in campaigns.

Dr. Renee Engeln, a body image researcher at Northwestern University, warns, "We have to watch out for messages that look positive, but actually reinforce old standards in sneaky ways. Pay attention to how images make you feel—your feelings are accurate signals about what's helpful and what isn't."

If you start to feel weighed down by comparison, step back. Social media is just one way to connect to body positivity—not the only way. A walk with a friend, time spent doing something you love, or writing down one thing you appreciate about your body can go a long way toward resetting your mindset.

Translating Inspiration into Daily Life: Practical Strategies for Self-Acceptance

Following body-positive influencers is a wonderful start, but translating inspiration into real self-acceptance involves daily decisions—big and small. It's one thing to double-tap a post about loving your body. It's quite another to turn off the inner critic when you look in the mirror before school or swim with friends.

One practical approach is adopting affirmations. Several influencers, including Danae Mercer and Ash Soto, credit self-talk as a turning point. Repeating phrases like, "My body deserves kindness," or "I am more than a number," each morning or night might sound silly at first, but science backs it up. Studies show regular positive affirmations can help train the brain to build self-esteem over time. The more you speak kindly to yourself, the more natural it becomes.

Another helpful practice is curating your environment. This means filling your world—not just your social media—with reminders of realistic beauty. You might hang up inspirational notes on your bedroom mirror, subscribe to magazines or shows that celebrate diversity, or join a supportive online group. The company you keep—in person and online—shapes your sense of self more than you might realize.

Dressing in ways that honor your comfort and style, rather than squeezing into a trend that feels wrong, is also powerful. When influencer and fashion designer Nicolette Mason started showcasing outfits that highlighted, rather than hid, her curves, she wrote, "For the first time, I dressed for myself—boldly, unapologetically. It changed everything about how I walked through the world." Wearing clothes that fit well and feel good can spark more confidence than any filter.

Self-care, too, becomes an act of resistance in a culture that profits off insecurity. This could be as simple as moving your body for joy, not punishment—dancing in your room, taking a walk for fresh air, or trying a new sport for fun. It might mean nourishing yourself with food you enjoy and that makes you feel strong, without guilt or shame attached. Celebrating the ways your body lets you move, create, hug, and laugh can reframe the story from "how I look" to "what I can do."

Journaling often helps people untangle difficult feelings about body image. You might write a letter to your younger self, listing everything you wish someone had told you about beauty and worth. Or you could keep a gratitude journal, focusing on qualities you love about yourself—inside and out.

Lastly, practicing gratitude is a powerful shift. Instead of criticizing a body part, try appreciating its function. Your legs might not look like a magazine editor's, but maybe they run you toward friends at lunchtime or kick powerfully in the pool. Your stretch marks might be evidence of growing taller, surviving puberty, or life's big changes. With practice, thanks can shout louder than criticism.

Support matters, too. Opening up to trusted friends, family members, or a counselor about your struggles can take away the shame. Sometimes, loved ones help us see beauty we can't recognize ourselves. And the more we speak about body image honestly, the more others feel safe to do the same.

Self-acceptance, like any meaningful habit, happens step-by-step. Some days will feel easier. Others might stretch your patience. But every small act of kindness toward yourself—whether that's ignoring a negative comment online, wearing clothes you love, or celebrating movement, not appearance—matters.

The legacy of body positive influencers is not just viral videos or hashtag trends. It's the way they plant seeds in millions of viewers—a reminder that joy, worth, and beauty aren't reserved for one kind of body, but belong to absolutely everyone.

Chapter 18

Most people know how it feels to wake up each morning with a to-do list that seems more like a steep mountain than a gentle hill. In these moments, life can appear demanding and relentless, as if it's all about making it to the end of each day with enough energy left to try again tomorrow. This state is often called "survival mode"—a way of moving through life with just enough momentum to get by, but not enough to truly enjoy the journey. Yet, there is a powerful difference between surviving and thriving, and, more importantly, a pathway from the first to the second. This journey starts with awareness.

Recognizing the Shift: Signs You're Ready to Move Beyond Survival Mode

At first, survival mode is like a protective shield. When stress feels overwhelming or change spins life in new directions, focusing on simple survival helps us cope. But as time goes on, the world can start to appear in color again instead of gray. Subtle signs emerge that suggest you're ready for something more than just scraping by.

Perhaps you notice that you're not as exhausted by the daily grind as you once were. Tasks that seemed impossible months ago now fit into your day with less strain. There may even be flashes of excitement about the future, or a spark of curiosity returning to the way you see your world.

Dr. Brené Brown, a researcher known for her work on vulnerability and courage, notes, "We're hardwired for connection, curiosity, and engagement." If your mind starts wandering toward new interests or you find yourself laughing a bit more freely, you're experiencing evidence of exactly what Dr. Brown describes—a readiness to move on from survival and into a richer, more connected life.

Another sign is the desire to make choices rather than feeling like life is simply happening to you. You notice options where once you only saw demands. Instead of rushing from task to task on autopilot, you begin pausing to think about what truly matters. This awareness itself is a small miracle.

And finally, the reappearance—or new arrival—of hope can be the strongest signal of all. According to data from the American Psychological Association, hope is among the most reliable indicators that someone is prepared to thrive rather than just survive.

When these feelings start bubbling to the surface, it might be tempting to ignore them or worry about whether they will last. But they are not figments of your imagination; instead, they are signposts pointing toward greater possibilities. Listening to them and gently nurturing their growth is the first step toward making the shift from surviving to thriving.

Reframing Daily Challenges as Opportunities for Growth

Moving toward thriving doesn't mean life suddenly becomes easy. It simply means you relate to life differently. One of the most powerful ways to support this shift is to see everyday challenges not as obstacles, but as teachers.

This doesn't require ignoring difficulties or pretending everything's fine when it isn't. Instead, it means asking, "What can I learn here?" For example, a teenager struggling with a difficult math class might at first see only frustration and failure. But as confidence grows, it becomes possible to look at the challenge as a chance to develop persistence, patience, or creative problem-solving.

Dr. Carol Dweck, the psychologist behind the "growth mindset" theory, has shown in years of research that how we interpret setbacks matters more than the setbacks themselves. Children and adults who view mistakes as chances to learn tend to achieve more, and—more importantly—enjoy the process.

Take Maya, a college freshman whose first semester

felt like one stumbling block after another. She missed deadlines, struggled to keep up with lectures, and failed a quiz she thought she had aced. In survival mode, Maya might have simply endured, telling herself she'd never measure up. But after a conversation with a professor who reminded her that all beginners stumble, Maya decided to view her difficulties as guideposts. Instead of hiding from her mistakes, she decided to study her missteps, asking herself what could be different next time—not to judge herself, but to learn.

Maya's story isn't unique. In fact, every day is dotted with little irritations or missteps that can become practice fields for growth. Maybe it's a difficult conversation with a loved one, a setback at work, or a misjudged decision. Thriving isn't about skipping over these moments, but meeting them with a sense of curiosity.

Imagine if you met frustration with a quiet, "What is this teaching me?" or handled a criticism with, "How could I use this to get better?" This simple change in thinking transforms the world into a series of invitations to grow, not just a parade of difficulties to endure.

The possibilities are sometimes surprising—like the time author J.K. Rowling said, "Rock bottom became the solid foundation on which I rebuilt my life." What once felt like absolute defeat can, with a shift in mindset, offer up the seeds of future confidence and wisdom.

Cultivating Confidence Through Small, Consistent Actions

Confidence is not a magical gift reserved for a lucky few. It is built, step by step, often in the smallest ways. When someone is moving from surviving to thriving, these small actions matter more than grand gestures.

Consider the story of Ben, an eighth grader who was terrified of speaking up in class. For months, he hid behind his textbooks, convinced that his voice wobbled and his answers were flawed. But Ben's teacher encouraged him to answer just one question each week, no more and no less. The first time, Ben felt his heart pound in his chest, and his voice was barely above a whisper. But his classmates smiled, and his teacher nodded approvingly. The following week, Ben answered another question, and each answer came a little easier. By the end of the semester, Ben was sharing his ideas more often and, more importantly, felt a surge of pride that carried over beyond the classroom.

Tiny actions build trust. Trust in yourself that "I can do hard things." Experts agree—psychologist Angela Duckworth, best known for her work on grit, points out that "enthusiasm is common. Endurance is rare." And endurance is fostered not by leaps, but by steady, repeated efforts.

Setting small, achievable goals creates momentum. For some people, it begins with making their bed each morning, or journaling for five minutes a day. For others, it may be raising their hand in class, or having one honest conversation a week. These are not grand milestones, but day-by-day, they stack up.

Research backs this up. A study published in the European Journal of Social Psychology found that it takes, on average, sixty-six days for a new behavior to become a habit. This isn't about perfection, but dedication. Missing a day does not mean failure. Instead, it's the return, again and again, that forges new habits and belief in one's own capacity.

Confidence grows in environments of self-compassion. If a mistake happens, gentle self-talk—"That was tough, but I'm still learning"—helps pave the way for trying again tomorrow. In this nurturing atmosphere, even setbacks become fuel for the journey forward.

Confidence isn't always flashy or loud. Often it grows quietly, like roots stretching under the soil, until one day, there's something strong enough to stand tall above the ground. Each small promise kept to oneself serves as a brick in the foundation of thriving.

Building Supportive Environments That Encourage Thriving

Thriving rarely happens in isolation. Even the most

self-motivated individuals find their progress strengthened by the people and spaces surrounding them. The environment you spend time in—whether at home, school, work, or with friends—can play an enormous role in nurturing (or stifling) the confidence you seek to anchor.

Sometimes this looks like surrounding yourself with people who believe in you, even on days you can't believe in yourself. Research from Stanford University found that having at least one supportive adult makes young people more likely to overcome adversity and thrive later in life.

Think of Serena, a high school sophomore who always dreamed of running track but doubted her abilities because no one in her family had ever been an athlete. Her coach, Ms. Patterson, took the time to notice her efforts. She gave Serena constructive feedback and honest praise, not empty compliments, helping her see that mistakes were part of everyone's learning curve. Over time, Serena's fear faded, replaced by a new sense of belonging—not just to the sport, but among teammates who pushed and cheered for her.

Physical environment matters, too. Consider carving out small spaces that inspire calm or creativity—a corner with a favorite chair and good lighting for reading, or a desk with personal mementos for studying. The presence of a tidy, welcoming spot can help signal to your brain that this is a place for growth and rest, not just endless chores.

Friend groups often shape how we feel about ourselves and what we believe is possible. If negativity, competition, or criticism dominate, confidence can dwindle. On the other hand, supportive circles—the kind that celebrate each other's wins and offer kind guidance after setbacks—help foster a sense of belonging and bolster the courage needed to step outside comfort zones.

This doesn't mean you need only "perfect" people around you. It means seeking—or becoming—the kind of person who lifts others up, models resilience, and encourages honest reflection. Social psychologist Dr. Amy Cuddy often remarks, "Tiny tweaks can lead to big changes." A supportive environment is built not through dramatic transformation but through consistent, caring actions over time.

If the current environment feels harsh or unsupportive, changing everything overnight is unrealistic. Sometimes, the first step is finding just one person, or one safe space, and starting to build outward from there. A positive environment is less about perfection and more about intention—a daily decision to create spaces, online or in person, where thriving feels possible.

Celebrating Progress and Sustaining Momentum

When moving from surviving to thriving, progress

can feel elusive—especially because it often happens gradually, almost invisibly, day after day. That's why taking the time to notice and celebrate achievements, no matter how small, is essential.

Celebration needn't be noisy or public. Sometimes, a quiet smile at the end of a tough day, a mental high-five, or a checkmark in a journal can be enough. The key is acknowledgement. Dr. Teresa Amabile of Harvard University has shown that even tiny wins can bring significant boosts to well-being and motivation. Her research on "The Progress Principle" found that people who recognized and celebrated small victories felt more engaged and productive than those who overlooked their advances.

Take Sarah, a single mother who once struggled to get out of bed most mornings. After deciding to tackle life one small change at a time, she celebrated each week she managed to cook a meal instead of ordering takeout—sometimes rewarding herself with an evening walk or a favorite book. These acts, simple yet meaningful, offered reminders that she was capable of change and worthy of joy.

Sustaining momentum means gently pushing forward, even when it's tempting to pause or backtrack. Everyone—including experts, athletes, and artists—has days when they feel they're moving in slow motion. Olympic gold medalist Simone Biles has shared in interviews that "progress is not always a straight line," and sometimes the smallest steps are the most important.

Part of sustaining momentum is recognizing that thriving is not about reaching one final destination. It's about experiencing growth in everyday life, repeatedly choosing curiosity over fear, compassion over criticism, and hope over helplessness.

As progress accumulates, new habits take root, and confidence becomes part of your daily rhythm. Challenges lose a little of their power to intimidate. Setbacks don't seem quite as final. The voice inside that once whispered, "I can't" grows a little quieter, replaced by one that softly insists, "Maybe I can."

The shift from surviving to thriving isn't about living a perfect, problem-free life. It's about greeting each new day as an opportunity—not for perfection, but for presence, growth, and confidence that you can keep moving forward, whatever the day may bring. Each sunrise is another chance to do just that.

Chapter 19

Our stories shape us in ways we often don't realize. From our earliest memories to the unexpected twists that life throws our way, the narrative we build around our experiences forms a bridge to ourselves and to those around us. You may think your life is ordinary, but the truth is, every journey carries its own magic. When you begin to see your story for what it truly is—a powerful tool for connection and transformation—you start to shine like a beacon for others seeking light.

Understanding the Power of Personal Narrative

There's something captivating about listening to someone's authentic story. Oprah Winfrey, a woman who built an empire on conversation and honesty, once said, "The greatest discovery of all time is that a person can change his future by merely changing his attitude." At the heart of that shift lies the story each of us chooses to tell about ourselves.

Stories are not just entertainment, or a way to pass the time; they are bearers of meaning. Social scientists have found that when people share personal experiences, listeners identify, empathize, and, in many cases, are moved to act. Research from Dr. Paul Zak at Claremont Graduate University shows the brain releases oxytocin—sometimes called the "love hormone"—when we hear compelling stories. This hormone is essential for connection and trust, making narrative a very real ingredient in building strong relationships.

When you reflect on your own life, notice the stories you tend to repeat. Which moments have you chosen to highlight? Are they tales of overcoming adversity, or shy recollections of near-misses and missteps? The stories we focus on become the threads that form our self-image. Dr. Dan McAdams, a leader in personality psychology, writes, "We are all storytellers, and our stories are our identities." The story you choose to tell about yourself is the foundation for who you are now, and who you might become.

Recognizing this is the first step in owning your story. It's not about having a fairytale background or heroic accomplishments; it's about finding power in your truth, even the messy, unfinished parts. A single detail from your day can be woven into a narrative that not only honors your experience, but also inspires someone else out of a struggle that feels eerily familiar.

For example, Maya Angelou, whose stories have inspired millions, once described how childhood trauma affected her voice—literally and figuratively.

For years, she was silent, believing her words could bring harm. Eventually, she found purpose in storytelling and turned pain into poetry, touching lives with her bravery. Her story reminds us that what feels broken can become the most meaningful chapter.

This isn't unique to the famous or the extraordinary. You can find people in every community who, through telling their truth, change the course of their own lives and those of others. Consider a local high school teacher, who shares with her students how she struggled with reading as a child. Instead of hiding her difficulties, she turns them into a source of encouragement, showing kids that difficulties do not have to define their future. That's the quiet power of personal narrative, working in real places, with real people.

Embracing Vulnerability to Create Genuine Connections

To be open about our stories, especially the imperfect, raw edges, requires vulnerability. And vulnerability is brave—not weak. Dr. Brené Brown, a research professor and bestselling author, has dedicated much of her career to exploring vulnerability and its role in connection. She often explains, "Vulnerability is the core, the heart, the center of meaningful human experiences." When you lower your guard, you create a space where others feel safe to do the same.

It's natural to want to hide your struggles, to paper over the sections of your life that didn't go as planned. Yet it's in these very moments—the ones that sting or embarrass—that the seeds of real connection are sown. When you tell a friend you were rejected by your first-choice college, or admit to feeling lost in a new job, you're sharing part of your humanity. These revelations strip away the masks we all wear, and in their place, trust and empathy begin to grow.

People respond to openness in remarkable ways. Take the story of Alex, a teenager who battled anxiety but was terrified of being judged. He finally opened up to a close friend. Instead of shrinking away, his friend nodded in understanding, sharing her own fears and worries. This simple act of honesty sparked a support system neither of them had expected. Their stories, once hidden, became the foundation for genuine friendship.

It can be easy to think vulnerability means telling everyone everything, all the time. Instead, it's about sharing in a way that's authentic and appropriate for the moment. There's strength in being honest about struggles, and discernment in choosing when, how, and with whom to share them.

For some people, starting small is the best way to build courage. Sharing a recent disappointment with someone trustworthy can ease you into more significant self-disclosure. Every act of openness encourages another, forming a chain reaction that can ignite transformation in a whole group, family, or classroom.

Authenticity, as Brené Brown notes, is the daily practice of letting go of who we think we're supposed to be and embracing who we are. When you let authenticity guide you, you become a magnet for others who crave realness. In a world that often values perfection, your vulnerability is a gift—it reassures people that being themselves is not just acceptable, but admired.

Transforming Challenges into Points of Inspiration

Every person faces difficulties, yet it's what we do with those experiences that determines the shape of our story. Hardships can feel like stumbling blocks, but over time, they can become powerful messages of hope.

Thomas Edison, known for inventing the light bulb, failed thousands of times before finding success. Instead of hiding those failures, he reframed them as lessons: "I have not failed. I've just found 10,000 ways that won't work." That attitude—the willingness to share not only achievements but also the entire journey—allows others to see the value in persistence and resilience.

Sometimes, the greatest inspiration comes from moments that looked like defeat. Consider the story of Bethany Hamilton, a professional surfer who lost an arm in a shark attack as a teenager. Instead of leaving surfing behind, she returned to the ocean and continued to compete, publicizing her journey in interviews and a memoir. Her openness about frustration, sadness, and determination moved countless others facing their own setbacks.

You do not need a headline-making struggle to inspire. Each challenge you face becomes an opportunity to offer perspective and hope. When you talk honestly about surviving a tough semester, caring for a loved one during illness, or working through family conflict, you shine a light on possible paths forward for someone going through a similar situation.

In fact, studies from Harvard Business School have shown that people are often more motivated by stories of struggle followed by growth than by stories of unbroken success. Seeing someone overcome obstacles reminds us that setbacks are not dead ends. Instead, they are invitations to try again, perhaps with greater wisdom and new tools.

Transforming hardship into inspiration does not mean glossing over the difficulties. Nobody expects you to spin suffering into instant positivity. Instead, it's about finding and sharing moments of learning, even if those lessons took root slowly, or are still growing. Sometimes, sharing that you're still in process—still making sense of things—is encouragement enough.

As people begin to see your perseverance, they may be empowered to face their own challenges with new resolve. It's important to celebrate the small victories that arise from difficult circumstances: a kind word received, a skill learned, or the simple decision to get up and try again. Even in unglamorous moments, inspiration can flourish if you are willing to acknowledge both the hardship and the hope.

Amplifying Your Impact: Sharing Your Story Responsibly

Telling your story is a powerful act, and with power comes responsibility. It's easy to get swept up in the excitement of being heard, but mindful storytelling considers who might be listening and how your words might affect them.

Responsible storytelling starts with honesty—both about your experiences and about the limitations of your perspective. No one has the full picture at all times. By admitting what you don't know, you actually build more trust with those around you. Dr. Marshall Ganz, a renowned organizer and lecturer at Harvard, teaches the idea of "Public Narrative," a framework that calls us to intertwine our story (the "story of self") with the "story of us." This helps your personal journey find resonance with communal values, bridging individual experience and collective meaning.

Maintaining privacy—yours and others'—is a vital part of storytelling. When you recount an event involving friends or family, it's respectful to consider their side. Would they be comfortable with you sharing their role in your narrative? Sometimes it's best to change details or ask for permission. Children, especially, deserve extra protection; what's cathartic for you might be deeply embarrassing or even harmful for someone else.

Clarity of purpose is another element of responsible storytelling. Ask yourself: Why am I sharing this? Am I seeking support, offering hope, or simply venting? Each reason is valid, but understanding your motive will help you avoid oversharing or unintentionally causing harm.

Tone matters as well. Many experts suggest taking care not to glamorize or normalize destructive behaviors. For example, when talking about mental health challenges, it's powerful to share the reality, but equally important to discuss the steps taken toward healing, whether they involve therapy, support from loved ones, or self-care routines.

Finally, responsible storytelling means being mindful of your audience. What feels appropriate with close friends may not be right for social media or public platforms. Social media can make it all too easy to broadcast stories to an audience wider than you intend. Once a story is out, it can't always be taken back. Choose your platforms thoughtfully and consider the reach of your words.

A story told with care, truth, and respect becomes a resource—not only for yourself, but for anyone searching for reassurance or guidance. Like a lighthouse guides ships away from rocky shores, a thoughtfully shared story can help others navigate their own rough seas.

Encouraging and Empowering Others to Share Their Own Journeys

Once you begin to own your story, an exciting shift happens. You inspire others to find their voices, too. This ripple effect can transform families, classrooms, organizations, and communities. One person's courage to speak out invites others to step forward.

The process starts with listening. Too often, storytelling is pictured as a solo act—a person standing at a microphone, alone in the spotlight. But real storytelling is interactive: a conversation, not a monologue. Be genuinely curious about the stories of those around you. Ask questions, offer your full attention, and honor the details that matter most to the teller.

Malala Yousafzai, Nobel laureate, survived violence and oppression and later became an international advocate for girls' education. Despite the danger and the scars she carries, Malala amplifies the voices of others, encouraging young people everywhere to share their experiences and visions. She once said, "When the whole world is silent, even one voice becomes powerful." Her words underline the importance of making space for every narrative, no matter how quiet or unpolished it may seem.

There are countless ways to make storytelling accessible. In some families, this means regular check-ins at the dinner table, offering everyone a chance to talk about their day. In schools, teachers can create safe spaces for students to write, speak, or create art based on personal experiences. Even a small group of friends can build rituals—like sharing a "high and low" from the week—to foster connection.

Sometimes, sharing begins with helping someone name their feelings or memories. For someone who has never seen themselves as a "storyteller," even simple prompts can unlock powerful narratives: What's a time you felt proud? Who has helped you through a tough moment? What's something about your culture or family that's important to you?

It's important to encourage at one's own pace. Not everyone is ready to share everything at once, and some stories remain unspoken for years. Offering respect for each person's journey means supporting their boundaries as well as their bravery.

Empowering others also means modeling graciousness for silences, as well as for revelations. When someone is met with patience and acceptance, it builds trust and confidence. Instead of pushing for more than someone is willing to give, hold space for whatever they are ready to say.

Community organizations and online platforms have recognized the transformative power of shared storytelling. Programs like The Moth and StoryCorps have inspired thousands to step up, microphone in hand, to speak their truth. The results are remarkable—teens telling stories of hope after loss; grandparents recalling immigration journeys; strangers discovering common ground. All it takes is one voice to spark a chain reaction.

Being a beacon is not about self-promotion. It's about lighting a path so others can see themselves more clearly. When you help someone find the courage to share, you are giving them the rare and precious gift of being witnessed. That acknowledgment can be the turning point between feeling invisible and believing you matter.

As you continue to own your story, keep in mind the responsibility you carry and the influence you wield. Sharing is always a balance—of truth and care, openness and respect—but the rewards ripple across lives in unpredictable, beautiful ways. It's not merely about standing out, but about reaching out, offering a steady light for those eager to find their way home.

Chapter 20

In the stillness of an early morning, when the world feels heavy and silent, there are moments when it seems almost impossible to feel good about ourselves. That quiet vulnerability—raw and honest—can be one of the most difficult places to exist. And yet, in those moments, true self-love is forged, not by accident, but by intention and repetition.

Self-love isn't just a concept we whisper to ourselves on difficult days. It's a foundation, a steady ground beneath our feet, laid down one brick at a time with every small decision to honor who we really are. In turning inward, we find the everlasting foundation—unshakeable, sturdy, weathered by our own hands. But how is such an unbreakable base built? It begins with a look back, a reflection on the path that brought us here.

Reflecting on the Journey: Revisiting Key Lessons in Self-Love

Have you ever walked through the woods and turned to see the winding path behind you? Each footprint, each twist and stumble, tells a story—a collection of choices and emotions, mistakes and breakthroughs. Self-love develops in a similar way: not in grand gestures, but in the accumulation of small, consistent, and sometimes imperfect actions.

Emily, a high school art teacher, remembers the moment she learned this. For years, she tied her self-worth to the evaluations she received from others. Praise made her soar; criticism crushed her spirit. After a particularly tough semester, she paused to review the pages of her journal. There, she discovered a pattern: on days she acted kindly to herself—whether through a hot cup of tea, a walk in the park, or simply forgiving herself quickly for a poor decision—she was able to cope with setbacks more easily.

Self-love, she realized, wasn't an outcome but a constant practice. It lives in the spaces between what happens to us and the ways we choose to respond to ourselves. Dr. Kristin Neff, one of the world's leading experts on self-compassion, reminds us, "Having compassion for yourself means that you honor and accept your humanness." That means it's not perfection that builds self-love, but understanding, forgiveness, and the willingness to try again.

Over the months, you may have noticed your own growth. Maybe, once, you avoided mirrors entirely, unable to meet your own gaze. Now, even on tough days, you're able to draw a breath and recount something you did well—a kind word spoken to a friend, a joke that made someone laugh, a simple act of courage. These are the bricks in your foundation.

Psychologists often describe self-love as a skill—a teachable, learnable way of caring for oneself. Just as we learn to ride a bike or solve an equation, self-love is practiced and refined over time. Researchers from the University of Waterloo found that people who practice self-kindness are better equipped to handle stress. The study's participants reported feeling more resilient after setbacks, not because they never struggled, but because they learned to reflect, forgive, and continue forward.

Reflection is not simply recognizing failures or achievements. It's about seeing the shades in between—the many moments in your life when you chose to encourage yourself even when it felt unnatural or uncomfortable. These quiet acts of self-kindness add up, shaping the person you are today.

As you look back over your own life, what are the moments that stand out—not for their triumphs, but for their honesty? Where did you offer yourself grace instead of judgment? Make space for these memories, because they are evidence: you have built something real and lasting.

Identifying and Honoring Your Core Values

Beneath every meaningful life sits a set of values—guiding lights that shape our decisions and whisper to us in moments of uncertainty. Core values are more than inspirational words written in a journal; they are living, breathing convictions that steer how we treat ourselves and others.

Years ago, author Brené Brown asked participants in her research to name their deepest values. Most thought it would be easy—surely, we know what matters most to us. Yet, as the exercise began, many found themselves grasping at a long list of admirable traits, unable to narrow them down. Brown recommends picking no more than two core values, for true clarity is born from focus.

Why is it so important to know—and honor—your core values? Because self-love feels hollow when it's not anchored in authenticity. If you believe in honesty but often find yourself pretending to be someone else to fit in, the gap between your true self and your behavior can grow uncomfortable. The same is true if you value kindness but are harsh with yourself when things go wrong.

Identifying your values takes honest reflection. Consider the moments you've been proudest—not just of what you accomplished, but of how you acted. Were you brave? Compassionate? Was it integrity that made you stand up for someone who was being bullied, or was it your creative problem-solving that inspired a group to collaborate? Often, our values reveal themselves most clearly during tough decisions or pivotal moments.

Once you've identified your values, honoring them becomes a new practice. Let's say you have decided that growth is one of your guiding principles. Each day, you might seek out opportunities to learn—reading for twenty minutes before bed, asking thoughtful questions, or trying a new skill. That decision might look small, but its consistency reinforces the idea that you are living authentically and loving yourself in the process.

Dr. Steven Hayes, founder of Acceptance and Commitment Therapy, says, "If you don't know what you value, you can't know who you are." And without knowing who you are at your core, self-love becomes just another performance—something you put on for show, rather than a deep, real truth you live each day.

Honoring your values, then, is a living demonstration of self-respect. It means aligning your actions with your beliefs, even when it's inconvenient or misunderstood by others. Over time, this alignment makes your foundation of self-love unshakeable, because it is built on a commitment to what truly matters most to you.

Let yourself take up the space your values deserve. Stand tall in them, especially when uncertainty arises. The more you do, the more confidence grows—not in your perfection, but in your authenticity.

Establishing Daily Rituals to Reinforce Self-

Acceptance

A house stands strong not because of the brick alone, but because of the rituals that keep it maintained—the sweeping of floors, the painting of walls, the gentle tightening of a loose hinge. In the architecture of self-love, daily rituals are the caretakers, ensuring the foundation remains sturdy and welcoming.

Some people imagine that affirming self-love requires elaborate routines—hour-long meditations, expensive spa days, or globe-spanning adventures of self-discovery. Yet, the science tells us otherwise. Dr. Barbara Fredrickson, professor of psychology at the University of North Carolina, finds that small, repeated acts of positive self-attention have far greater impact than grand gestures done rarely. Micro-moments of kindness towards ourselves add up, rewiring our brains and reshaping our habits.

Consider the ritual of a morning affirmation. Maybe you wake, stretch your arms toward the ceiling, and whisper a simple promise to yourself. "Today, I treat myself with care." These words aren't magic—they're intention. Over time, as brain researchers note, repeated positive suggestions can carve new, healthier neural pathways, making self-acceptance easier and more natural.

Or take the practice of gratitude journaling. According to a study from the Greater Good Science Center at UC Berkeley, people who jot down three things they are thankful for every day report higher levels of happiness and self-esteem. The trick isn't the length of the list, but the regularity. It's the quiet moment of attention—"I appreciate my perseverance today," or "I'm proud that I reached out to a friend when I needed help"—that deepens your self-connection.

Rituals can be playful, too. Thirteen-year-old Jayden started a "cool things about me" jar after a particularly rough year at middle school. Each evening, he scribbled a quick note for something he liked about himself: "I made someone laugh," or "I tried hard in math, even if I didn't get the answer." At the end of the year, Jayden dumped out the jar and read each piece of paper. Seeing his strengths in his own handwriting filled him with a pride that no test score ever could.

Mindfulness is another small but mighty practice. Just taking five minutes to sit quietly, breathing deeply, and observing your thoughts without judgment can work wonders. "Mindfulness helps us step back from our inner critic," says psychologist Dr. Susan David, "and recognize our feelings for what they are—just feelings." Consistent mindfulness has been shown to reduce anxiety and increase self-compassion.

Some daily rituals involve gentle movement—yoga, stretching, or a walk outside, simply noticing the sky and the feel of the wind. Taking care of your body, not as a punishment for what it is not, but as a celebration of all it can do, transforms your relationship with yourself.

Let rituals shift and evolve. There will be days when a kind note to yourself is enough, and others when you might need a quiet cup of tea, a favorite song, or the reminder of an encouraging text from a loved one. The real magic lies in the commitment—the daily choice to show up for yourself, regardless of your mood or the circumstances swirling outside.

Ultimately, it is these steady, repeated actions that reinforce your belief in your own worthiness. Each one whispers, "You matter, every day."

Sustaining Growth: Navigating Setbacks with Compassion

Building an unshakeable foundation doesn't mean storms won't come. The truth is, even with the strongest self-love, there will be days when doubts creep in, or mistakes seem overwhelming. During these moments, the difference between crumbling and growing comes down to compassion—an ability to meet yourself, flaws and all, with softness instead of scorn.

Consider the story of Mina, a college freshman away from home for the first time. She had always been a high achiever, proud of her straight A's and busy schedule. But when her first semester became a struggle, grades slipped and anxiety mounted. Mina began to criticize herself mercilessly, replaying every misstep as proof that she had failed.

A counselor gently encouraged her to imagine how she would treat a close friend in the same situation. "I'd tell her she was trying her best and that one rough patch didn't erase all the things she'd accomplished," Mina admitted. The counselor's response was simple: "Why not offer that same grace to yourself?"

It sounds easy, but for many, self-compassion feels unnatural. Research from the University of Texas at Austin found that practicing self-compassion predicted greater emotional resilience and lower levels of depression. Rather than being self-indulgent or making excuses, it's about offering yourself permission to be imperfect.

When setbacks come, the first instinct of the inner critic is often to shout. "You messed up again!" "See, you'll never get it right!" And yet, clinical psychologist Dr. Kristin Neff encourages a different approach: "Speak to yourself as you would to someone you love—with patience, empathy, and encouragement." Even phrasing like, "This is hard right now, but I can get through it," or "I'm not alone in feeling this way," can change the tone of your self-talk.

There are practical ways to practice self-compassion in the face of setbacks. Allow yourself a short break—a walk, a chat with a supportive friend—or write yourself a letter from the perspective of someone who cares deeply for you. Reflect on the lessons to be learned, without letting shame take over.

It's helpful to remember that progress is rarely a straight line. Olympic gold medalist Simone Biles once said, "I'd rather regret the risks that didn't work out than the chances I didn't take at all." Even the most successful individuals face failure and self-doubt. The difference is in how they recover: with an open heart, a willingness to learn, and a refusal to let one mistake define everything.

Over time, setbacks can become some of your greatest teachers, revealing the parts of yourself that need gentler attention and deeper understanding. Approaching yourself with compassion in these times isn't weakness—it's a sign of maturity and wisdom.

Allow yourself space to process tough moments without judgment. Cry if you need to, stomp in frustration, or spend an hour wrapped in a blanket binge-watching your favorite show. Then, when you are ready, step back onto your foundation—grounded by the rituals and values you have honored, and by a growing belief that you are worthy of kindness, especially from yourself.

Embracing a Lifelong Commitment to Yourself

In a world that is always changing, there will be

pressures to adapt, to change focus, or to chase after an ever-shifting idea of what's "enough." Through all those seasons and changes, there is one constant: your relationship with yourself. This is not a single choice made once, but a daily, lifelong commitment to honor who you are and who you are becoming.

Committing to yourself doesn't require grand declarations or infallible willpower. It unfolds in the quiet acts of coming back, again and again, to the practices that nurture you. Just as an oak tree grows rings with every passing year—weathering wind, drought, and rain—you can continue to add depth to your foundation with each season of your life.

Experts agree that one of the most significant predictors of long-term happiness is self-acceptance. A 2014 study published by the British Psychological Society found that self-acceptance is a powerful predictor of psychological well-being, more so than either career success or financial stability. The researchers noted that most people spent far less time working on self-acceptance than on any other happiness factor; yet, those who actively practiced it benefitted the most.

Think of this commitment as a partnership with yourself—a mutual agreement to show up, to listen, to forgive mistakes, and to celebrate victories, large and small. On some days, this will feel effortless; on others, it will require everything you have. The key is that you keep choosing, over and over, to treat yourself with love.

Role models often inspire us with the ways they maintain this commitment. Mister Rogers, beloved television host and gentle advocate for children everywhere, once said, "Love isn't a state of perfect caring. It is an active noun, like 'struggle.' To love someone is to strive to accept that person exactly the way he or she is, right here and now." The same principle holds true for loving yourself. It is not something you attain and then hold forever, untouched—it is something you work at, with patience and persistence.

As life shifts, so will your needs, dreams, and even your values. The rituals that served you at sixteen may not fit at thirty. The ways you honored your body, mind, and spirit before school might evolve as work, family, health, and new challenges arise. This is not a sign of failure, but of growth. The everlasting foundation of self-love allows room for change, for new beginnings, and for continued learning.

Whenever you feel unsteady, when doubt or fear reemerges, remember the work you have already done. Reflection, authenticity, daily rituals, compassion—they are all threads woven into the fabric of your life. Some days, the weave will feel loose. On others, it will be tight and strong.

Commitment to yourself means continuing the conversation between who you are and who you yet hope to become. It means asking the difficult questions and celebrating the little victories. And most of all, it means never giving up on yourself, no matter how many false starts or tough chapters appear along the way.

The foundation of self-love, once built, doesn't guarantee a life free from pain or struggle. What it offers instead is a steady place to return—a well-worn path back to yourself—both when the world feels bright and when the night feels endless. In these returns, in this ongoing care, your foundation becomes truly everlasting.

As you move through future days, hold close the knowledge that self-love is not selfish, nor is it fragile. It is active, dynamic, continually shaped by your choices and your courage. Let your foundation be a promise: a whispered affirmation, a strong perimeter, a place inside yourself that will not waver, no matter what comes. In honoring yourself, day by day and year by year, you create something unshakeable: a self-love that is boundless and built to last.

Manufactured by Amazon.ca
Bolton, ON